Ethnocentrism in Foreign Policy

Ethnocentrism in Foreign Policy

Can We Understand the Third World?

Howard J. Wiarda

American Enterprise Institute for Public Policy Research
Washington and London

Howard J. Wiarda is a resident scholar of the American Enterprise Institute and the director of its Center for Hemispheric Studies. He is also a professor of political science at the University of Massachusetts, Amherst.

Library of Congress Cataloging in Publication Data

Wiarda, Howard J., 1939–
    Ethnocentrism in foreign policy: Can we understand the Third World?

    Bibliography: p.
    1. Developing countries—Foreign relations—United
States. 2. United States—Foreign relations—Developing countries. 3. United States—Foreign relations—
1945- . 4. Ethnocentrism. I. Title.
D888.U6W53 1984   327.73   84–28267

ISBN 0–8447–3569–8

AEI Studies 414   96402

Printed in the United States of America

Contents

Foreword

With this study Howard J. Wiarda, resident scholar at AEI and director of our Center for Hemispheric Studies, begins another new and innovative research project. The project deals with the newer ideas and models of modernization and development emanating from the Third World. It suggests that American social science and, by extension, U.S. foreign policy toward the Third World, is based heavily on the experiences of Western Europe and North America and therefore is often incapable of understanding or coping realistically with Third World areas whose histories and experiences are quite different from our own.

This project is funded in part by a major grant to our Center for Hemispheric Studies from the Mellon Foundation. This publication is a preliminary and exploratory statement of a larger project that we plan to complete in the next two years. The present study, which examines the conceptual and theoretical terrain, sets forth the main ideas of the project in preliminary fashion. The larger book that we plan to produce will have major substantive chapters on all the key Third World and Non-Western areas: Latin America, Africa, the Middle East, South and Southeast Asia, China, and Japan.

This project is only one of many in an ambitious research agenda being carried out by our Center for Hemispheric Studies. Other activities now under way include a project on U.S.–Mexican relations, a study of how Central America copes with crisis and upheaval, U.S. relations with the Southern Cone countries, the impact of Grenada on revolutionary prospects in Central America and the Caribbean, a project on the role of the state in Latin American development, a study of social and political change in Southern Europe and its implications for U.S. policy, a project on transitions to democracy in Iberia and Latin America, studies of Brazilian and Venezuelan development, and a project on family planning in Latin America. In addition, our center conducts a vigorous program of conferences, guest speakers, seminars, briefings, and lectures.

The ideas presented here are provocative and critical but also nonpartisan. Professor Wiarda suggests that almost all our social sciences of development are based on a model of change derived from Western Europe and the United States. Our foreign policy programs, whether in the areas of agrarian reform, military assistance, human rights, economic aid, democratization, and so on, are based on the same Western experiences. But Howard Wiarda argues that because these are often ethnocentric assumptions, they lead us to misunderstand the dynamics of many Third World areas and they lead American foreign policy toward these areas in directions that too often produce unanticipated and harmful consequences. He suggests a fundamental reexamination of the assumptions of U.S. policy toward the Third World.

It is a challenging argument with major implications for U.S. policy.

WILLIAM J. BAROODY, JR.
President
American Enterprise Institute

1
Introduction

The Problem: Ethnocentrism and American Foreign Policy

The Third World, viewed collectively by regional blocs or in terms of individually important nations (Argentina, Brazil, Egypt, India, Indonesia, Iran, Mexico, Nigeria, the Philippines, Venezuela, Vietnam), has become increasingly important to the United States in the past twenty-five years and has become a major focus of U.S. foreign policy. Yet it is also the area that we know and comprehend the least and where American policy has produced its most notorious gaffes and failures.

The Third World has become increasingly important to us economically. We now trade more with the Third World, including the Middle East and Latin America, than with Western Europe and Japan *combined*. In addition, most of our foreign policy crises in recent years have involved the Third World: Southeast Asia, the Middle East, the Horn of Africa, Southern Africa, Central America, and the Caribbean. Militarily, politically, strategically, we now need the Third World almost as much as it needs us.[1]

The thesis of this small volume is that at the heart of our foreign policy problems in the Third World, explaining why policy so often flounders or ends up on the shoals, is a fundamental lack of understanding and empathy about the Third World and Third World areas and countries. More specifically, we argue that at the root of our foreign policy dilemmas in these areas is a deeply ingrained American ethnocentrism, an inability to understand the Third World on its own terms, an insistence on viewing it through the lenses of our own Western experience, and the condescending and patronizing attitudes that such ethnocentrism implies. Embedded deeply in the American ethos, this ethnocentrism is part of our educational system and is reflected in the social science literature on development. It is also inherent in virtually all our policy initiatives: economic aid, military assistance, human rights and democracy, and the effort to initiate and

1

help implement agrarian reform, to name a few among many. The questions explored here are why this American ethnocentrism is so deeply ingrained, how that ethnocentrism affects foreign policy, and what—if anything—can be done about.

Discussion

The present study is a preliminary statement of a larger project currently under way at the American Enterprise Institute for Public Policy Research. The two following chapters written earlier by the author form the general theoretical background for the larger study. The first is an analysis and critique of the ethnocentrism of the literature and social sciences of development. It shows why policy based upon ethnocentric assumptions so often goes wrong. The second essay discusses preliminarily the new concepts and models of development emanating from the Third World itself. In the larger project of which this is a part, we plan to refine the general theoretical statement and include chapters on the major developmental models and approaches emanating from each Third World area.

Although the critique offered here is strong, it is meant to be nonpartisan. Both Democratic and Republican administrations have frequently exhibited the same ethnocentrism, the same appalling ignorance of Third World areas, the same patronizing and superior attitudes, the same inability to countenance models of development other than our own, and the same insistence that we know best for the Third World. At times a more liberal or a more conservative approach to development may prevail, but what is striking to long-time observers is that both these approaches derive from a uniquely American model that has but limited utility and applicability in the Third World.

The ground being plowed and sifted here is new ground, and the issues are controversial. These ideas challenge numerous established beliefs and call for a fundamental reexamination of major U.S. foreign policy programs. We argue that most such programs are so closely based on the North American–West European model of development that they are largely inapplicable in the Third World, where the conditions, culture, institutions, and practices are quite different from our own.

Not only is our own developmental model of limited relevance in these areas, but it may be downright harmful to the basic goals of U.S. policy in securing stable, functional, and friendly governments. We emphasize that the United States must be receptive to the growth of indigenous Third World institutions and developmental models and even encourage them. We see not one or two (capitalist or Communist, democratic or totalitarian), but many routes to development; we believe that, however inchoate, the theme of "finding our own path" is becoming universal throughout the Third World. Furthermore, we argue that it behooves the United States to comprehend, perhaps show some sympathy for—maybe even accommodate and assist—these new trends. We should not stand unalterably opposed to them or insist our way is the only way and thus be surprised and humiliatingly defeated, as in Iran, when our own preferred model and route to development are repudiated.

The ideas presented here are controversial not only because they challenge many deeply held assumptions of the social sciences and of our development assistance programs, but also because they seemingly run counter to many long-established American beliefs. We really believe, as a nation and a political culture, that our institutions are the best and most developed that mankind has devised, that we can export our institutions to less-favored lands, and even that we have a moral duty to do so. That missionary spirit of bringing the benefits of our civilization to the developing nations is very strong in America. It goes back to our Puritan and other Judeo-Christian forebears, it was strong among the Founding Fathers who wanted to teach Latin America about electing good men, and it is expressed in Woodrow Wilson's naive faith that we could "make the world safe for democracy." That spirit is also reflected in John F. Kennedy's Peace Corps and Alliance for Progress, in Jimmy Carter's campaign for human rights, and in Ronald Reagan's effort to promote democracy and laissez-faire economic enterprise in Central America. This ethos is deeply ingrained, it is of historic duration, and it crosses all partisan and ideological lines.

Another American ethos, however, is also deeply ingrained. It suggests that we take local institutions realistically on their own terms, rather than through our own rose-colored glasses; that we respect existing institutions rather than seeking to sweep them away and thus creating the potential for confusion and chaos; that we seek not to impose our preferred (but in their context not always entirely appropriate) ways on others; that we have some Burke-like respect for history, including other peoples' histories. And that finally, in accordance with this attitude, we practice a considerable degree of restraint, tolerance, and laissez faire toward other nations' institutions—as we have long done with regard to our domestic economy and politics. We may still be able to assist in Third World areas and to suggest and even push for the outcomes we prefer. That can be done, however, not by imposition but only with some modesty and deference, genuinely

3

respecting the nations and local institutions with which we deal. We can suggest and prod, but heavy-handed interventionism and an attitude that we know best or that our institutions are superior simply will no longer do in most of the Third World.

Implications for Foreign Policy

These essays suggest that the crux of our difficulties in understanding Third World nations is our Eurocentrism—our belief that the developmental experience of Western Europe and North America can be repeated, even imitated (albeit belatedly) in the Third World. The models that we use, with regard to economic development, social change, or political modernization, all derive from this Euro-American experience. Hence we are ill-equipped to comprehend other regions whose ethos, institutions, and history (Islamic, tribalist, Buddhist, Confucian, or patrimonialist in various forms) are fundamentally different from our own.

Not only do policy prescriptions based on our own developmental experience and often applied indiscriminately to Third World nations go frequently astray, but our educational system does not prepare us to grasp fully why that is so. To a considerable degree the United States remains (about 30 percent of our population, the surveys tell us) an isolationist nation, and our experience abroad or training in foreign languages and cultures is quite limited. Our educational system is based almost exclusively on the liberal arts, which of course means the Euro-American tradition. In this tradition we generally only touch in limited ways on the Third World. This is not to condemn a liberal arts education—far from it—but it is to note the biases that this focus builds into our understanding of the world. If the liberal arts are, as suggested here, really an area study, lending themselves to assumptions that have particular rather than universal application, and if those assumptions are the ones on which we base much of our development literature as well as public policy, then it is small wonder that our initiatives in the Third World so often produce unanticipated consequences. It is not just our general educational system, however, that leaves us ill-prepared to understand Third World areas, but the kind of area-studies training provided our diplomats sent abroad is also woefully inadequate for them to comprehend the cultures, societal mores, and political dynamics of the countries to which they are sent.

The problem is not just an educational system that fails to equip us to understand non-Western areas; the problem lies deep in the American ethos and political culture. We are fundamentally a liberal,

4

republican, and democratic nation and, with some qualifications, have always been so. The question, as posed by Louis Hartz,[2] is whether a country born free as we were—that is, without a feudal or strongly patrimonialist past—can *ever* understand other nations not so blest. The answer, unfortunately, seems to be no.

These essays call for a thorough reexamination of many social science assumptions about the way nations change and modernize, about the development literature with which a whole generation and more of scholars and foreign affairs specialists have grown up, and about the policies based on these assumptions and literature. For example, a great deal of our economic assistance program aimed at the developing nations is still based, more implicitly than explicitly by now, on the 1960 book by W. W. Rostow, *The Stages of Economic Growth*,[3] a key book that helped shape the Alliance for Progress and all subsequent U.S. aid efforts. Rostow's position was strongly reinforced in other economic and sociological writings of the time, chiefly Kennedy liberals who had a strong hand in designing the Alliance for Progress—John Kenneth Galbraith, Robert Heilbroner, Lincoln Gordon, C. E. Black, Max Millikan, and Seymour M. Lipset.[4]

At this point, a quarter century later, the Agency for International Development is no longer quite so mesmerized by the Rostow categories, and its emphases have gone through various ups and downs: infrastructure growth, community development, basic human needs, free market development, and the like. But what is striking is the degree to which the Rostowian assumptions still hold: that there are "stages" of growth; that Europe and America provide the model; that the process is inevitable, unilinear, universal, and irreversible. All our experience in Third World countries in the past twenty-five years, however, leads to quite different conclusions: that the process is not necessarily inevitable, that decay and disintegration as well as growth may occur, that the Euro-American experience is not global but particular, that there are many routes to development and not one, that the social and political concomitants that are supposed to follow from economic growth do not in fact often follow, and that our experience is only of limited utility for the rest of the world.[5] Hence we have this curious situation where the old assumptions no longer hold, yet policy continues to be based in large part on them because of both bureaucratic and intellectual inertia and because we can find no suitable substitute.

Here we suggest that foreign policy toward the Third World in virtually all its aspects requires a fundamental reexamination. One can go down the list of U.S. policy initiatives, literally from top to bottom, and one finds that virtually all items are based on a Euro-

American model of dubious applicability in the Third World. This is not to say one should be against all these policies but only that their assumptions need to be reexamined, their relevance and prospects for success carefully weighed, and, where necessary, changes introduced.

Agrarian reform, for example, is based on the model of a medium-sized, middle-class, family-based, civically conscious yeoman farmer that may still apply in rural Wisconsin but seems of limited usefulness in Latin America. Our efforts to instill professionalism in many Third World armed forces are also based on an American model, one of strict segregation between the civilian and the military spheres, which simply does not apply in most Third World nations. Community Development has been superimposed on highly centralized code-law countries where the entire history has been to look to the central government for direction. The model of labor relations brought by the AFL-CIO to the Third World is based on a U.S. framework of nonpolitical collective bargaining that applies only partially in these other areas.[6]

The list of wrong, misleading, and ethnocentric assumptions can easily be expanded. Much of our economic assistance derives from the idea that greater affluence will lead to a larger middle class and that this new middle class will be moderate and pragmatic just like ourselves. The evidence, however, indicates that the middle classes in Latin America and elsewhere behave and act differently from that in the United States and are not likely to be a bastion of stability, democracy, and progress. Our efforts to forge a strong human rights policy in recent years, however laudable, have been based wholly on Western criteria and definitions, which are not always universally accepted except in a ritualistic sense and which do not convey the same meanings or hold the same importance in many Third World nations. Likewise, our recent efforts to export democracy are grounded entirely on U.S. understandings and institutional forms of democracy. Even terms like "capitalism," "private enterprise," and the like carry connotations in Japan, as well as in many Third World areas, quite different from our own.[7]

Understandably, we may have to use these terms politically in very simplified form because that is how policy proposals are able to get public support and pass Congress. But such usage often involves a trap as well. Let us take U.S. policy toward El Salvador as an example. We are in favor of democracy in El Salvador not only because it is intrinsically good but also because that helps the administration defuse congressional opposition and gain popular support. The trap for policy, however, is that our democracy agenda may not work, democracy may be overthrown, and we may have to face the reality of another repressive military regime. But if democracy should fail or be overthrown, we might still have to support the succeeding government, however undemocratic, because our nation's interests are affected. Favoring democracy is thus both an opportunity and a potential trap for policy. My own view is that we can favor a strong human rights policy and a policy in support of democracy, but that we must be very sure of what we are doing, accept the requirement to adapt our categories and prescriptions to particular Third World situations, and recognize the need to exercise restraint, prudence, and considerable forbearance in these matters.[8]

Agenda for the Future

The proposal put forth briefly here, to be developed at full length in our larger study, is that we must not only adapt our Euro-American models and understandings to quite different Third World contexts, but that the models derived from our Western experience and used in part are not universal. They have limited applicability in the Third World. Hence we must be prepared to accept and deal with an Islamic social science of development, an African social science of development, a Latin American social science of development, and so on. At the least we need to be very careful in suggesting what of the Euro-American experience of change is universal and what is not. More ambitiously, we need to know whether we can blend and reconcile what is useful, relevant, and *global* in the Western experience with the newer ideologies and developmental formulas, largely indigenous, originating in the Third World. The cry of "let us do it our way" is virtually unanimous in the Third World, and the insistence by these nations on fashioning their own models of development—as well as our response to this—is likely to be the next great frontier in the social sciences. As viewed here, however, and in the larger study on which we are working that will contain a full-length treatment of all the major Third World areas, the foreign policy implications are certain to be critical as well.

Notes

1. For elaboration, see Howard J. Wiarda, "Cancún and After: The United States and the Developing World," *PS*, vol. 15 (Winter 1982), pp. 40–48.
2. Louis Hartz, *The Liberal Tradition in America* (New York: Harcourt, Brace and World, 1955).
3. W. W. Rostow, *The Stages of Economic Growth* (Cambridge: Cambridge University Press, 1960).

4. See, for example, Robert Heilbroner's *The Great Ascent: The Struggle for Economic Development in Our Time* (New York: Harper and Row, 1963); Seymour M. Lipset's *Political Man: The Social Bases of Politics* (Garden City, N.J.: Doubleday, 1960); C. E. Black's *The Dynamics of Modernization: A Study in Comparative History* (New York: Harper and Row, 1966); and especially Max Millikan and W. W. Rostow's *A Proposal: Key to an Effective Foreign Policy* (New York: Harper, 1957), which had a major impact on policy at the time.

5. Some other writings by the author on this theme include *Politics and Social Change in Latin America: The Distinct Tradition* (Amherst: University of Massachusetts Press, 1982) and *Corporatism and National Development in Latin America* (Boulder, Colo.: Westview Press, 1981).

6. For a fuller discussion, see Howard J. Wiarda, "At the Root of the Problem: Conceptual Failures in U.S.–Central American Relations," in Robert Leiken, ed., *Central America: Anatomy of Conflict* (New York: Pergamon Press, 1984), 259–78.

7. Chalmers Johnson, "The Institutional Foundation of Japanese Industrial Policy," in Claude Barfield and William Schambra, eds., *The Politics of Industrial Policy* (Washington, D.C.: American Enterprise Institute, forthcoming); see also the collected essays in *Human Rights and U.S. Human Rights Policy* (Washington, D.C.: American Enterprise Institute, 1982); and Howard J. Wiarda, "Can Democracy Be Exported? The Quest for Democracy in United States Latin America Policy," in Kevin Middlebrook and Carlos Rico, eds., *The United States and Latin America* (tentative title, Pittsburgh: University of Pittsburgh Press, forthcoming).

8. For further argument, see Howard J. Wiarda, *In Search of Policy: The United States and Latin America* (Washington, D.C.: American Enterprise Institute, 1984).

2

The Ethnocentrism of the Social Sciences: Implications for Research and Policy

Western modernization has been accompanied throughout by a particular intellectual construction of that experience, prompted by moral or reforming impulses often presented in the guise of scientific generalizations.

REINHARD BENDIX

The proposition advanced here is that the vast bulk of our social science findings, models, and literature, which purport to be universal, are in fact biased, ethnocentric, and not universal at all. They are based on the narrow and rather particular experiences of Western Europe (actually a much smaller nucleus of countries in central and northwest Europe) and the United States, and they may have little or no relevance to the rest of the world. A growing number of scholars, particularly those who have had long research experience in the so-called developing nations, have now come to recognize this fact. Among others, new efforts are being made to reexamine the very "Western" experience on which so many of our social science "truths" and models have been based. Because these verities are still widely believed, however, by many scholars and policy makers alike, the ethnocentric biases and assumptions undergirding them need to be examined and their implications for research and policy explored.[1]

The influences that come together to push these concerns to the surface at this time are several, including continued stupefaction at many scholarly colleagues who know better or should know better yet persist in believing (though not always explicitly saying so) that what's good for Western Europe and the United States of America (or perhaps Taiwan, South Korea, Puerto Rico, or other nations where

This essay was written while the author was a Visiting Scholar at the Center for International Affairs, Harvard University. Research and writing were aided by a Senior Fellowship from the National Endowment for the Humanities. An earlier version of this chapter appeared in *The Review of Politics*, vol. 43, no. 2 (April 1981), pp. 163–197.

9

most development strategies were first tried out) must necessarily be good for Ecuador, Angola, or the Philippines; amazement at the condescending, patronizing, and superior attitudes that both scholars and high public officials (I am thinking particularly of former President Carter's "Montezuma's revenge" crack while on a state visit to Mexico) have toward Third World countries and peoples; consternation at our lack of comprehension of many Third World political movements, which we seldom understand or have much sympathy for; wonderment over the fact that U.S. scholars and policy makers are surprised when their misconceived programs fail to work or produce unanticipated consequences in the developing nations; bemusement that the great models in which many social scientists are true believers are increasingly revealed as having only limited predictive or explanatory power when applied in non-Western contexts; and a renewed series of research experiences abroad where the author had the opportunity to observe both the inadequacy of the Western social science and policy models *and* the growing assertiveness of indigenous ones with which we are almost entirely unacquainted.The present paper may thus be considered something of a personal response to some perceived major misdirections in the social sciences and in foreign policy, as well as a serious and scholarly effort to offer a critique on these and suggest new directions.

Not all the social sciences, of course, are equally guilty of the biases and ethnocentrism when confronting foreign cultures that we have ascribed to them. Sociology, with its universalist assumptions and the way in which most sociology departments are staffed, by subject area rather than by geographic or cultural area—seems to be the worst offender, giving rise to analysis that is often more wishful than based on the actual processes or institutions of the society or culture studied. Political science and economics may be only slightly less ethnocentric, however; and it is on these three disciplines that the following analysis concentrates. Anthropology, particularly cultural anthropology, has been more sympathetic to the need to take foreign societies on their own terms and in their own contexts rather than through the supposedly universalist perspective derived from the Western European and U.S. experience. Fifty years ago anthropologists went through their great debate concerning cultural relativism that is now about to occur in the other social sciences. Anthropologists, however, also have their biases and particularly as they, too, have turned to the examination of whole national systems and international links, the familiar prejudices have appeared there as well. Comparative psychology is such a new field that one might hope, without being unduly optimistic, it will be able to avoid the mistakes of the other social sciences. While there are thus degrees of bias and ethnocentrism in the social sciences, itself a topic deserving further careful research, all of them seem sufficiently narrow, particular, and parochial to profit from a reexamination of their basic assumptions.

The Nature of the Western Biases

To most of us a liberal arts education is something familiar, comfortable, an integral part of our intellectual upbringing. It shapes our thinking, our attitudes, and our intellectual preconceptions. However much our liberal arts heritage is celebrated, nonetheless, we must also recognize the biases inherent in that approach. Indeed, it may be that it is the very nature of our liberal arts focus that lies at the heart of our present dilemma and of our incomprehension of Third World nations. For as now structured, liberal arts education is essentially *Western* education, the Greco-Roman and Judeo-Christian traditions and European history, from which derive a set of concepts, ethics, and governing norms and experiences that have their basis in the Western background and that may have little reference to or applicability in other global areas. Although it is understandable that those who inhabit the West should structure their educational system as an appreciation of their own history and culture, we must also recognize such training for what it is: traditional liberal arts education is essentially the original "area study" program.[2]

Our concepts of justice, fair play, good government, progress, and development are similarly Western concepts. The latter two terms imply a certain unilinearism and inevitability in the evolution of man's social and political institutions. The former three imply some shared expectations about the social and political institutions and concomitants that are supposed to follow from industrialization and economic development. So long as we could divide the world into two parts, Western and non-Western, and so long as we assumed, à la Hegel, Marx, or W. W. Rostow, that the non-Western world would inevitably follow the same developmental path as the West ("the developed world shows to the less developed the mirror of its own future"),[3] our social science assumptions rested easily and comfortably. By this point, however, it is abundantly clear that these conditions no longer, if they ever did, apply. The world cannot be so simply divided, and it seems obvious that the developmental experience of today's emerging nations cannot repeat or mirror the experience of Western Europe. Our social science assumptions, based so heavily on the European experience, therefore require close reexamination as well.

Not only are our liberal arts traditions and hence our social sci-

11

ence assumptions Western, but they are also based strongly on metaphorical concepts. The great danger in the present context is that we have both reified our metaphorical constructs, failing to keep clear the difference between metaphor and reality, *and* extended what are essentially Western metaphors to the rest of the world where they neither fit nor have much meaning. Concepts like progress, development, stages of growth or modernization are metaphors, poetic devices that have some relations to reality but are not to be confused with the real thing.[4] Among AID administrators and many students of social and political change, however, development and modernization have been given real, flesh-and-blood attributes and have become measurable and quantifiable—so much so that in some writings on the subject and in many U.S. assistance programs, these concepts and the models derived from them have been treated as actually existing realities and as concrete policy programs. What are at best abstractions and ideal creations have been given real life characteristics with precise indicators for their measurement.

One of the contentions of this essay is that such concepts as development or modernization must be re-recognized for what they are: metaphors, poetic figures, shorthand tools, abstractions that have some importance in defining, outlining, or describing reality but that should not be mistaken for reality itself. Not only are they metaphorical devices with all the limitations for describing reality that implies, but they are *Western* metaphors, which may or may not (most likely the latter) have relevance to the non-Western world. Let us examine these propositions in terms of three major disciplines of particular importance, both to the study of development and to our understanding of the Western biases therein: political theory, political sociology, and political economy.

Political Theory. As taught in our usual history-of-political-thought courses and seminars, political theory demonstrates all the biases previously mentioned. It is prejudiced in favor of exclusively Western perspectives; it is narrowly ethnocentric and particularistic rather than universalistic; it seeks to show a unilinear and "progressive" development toward "modernity"; it favors some theories and is opposed to others; and it has little relevance to the developing nations.[5]

Most political theory courses spend a week or two on the pre-Socratics and then move quickly to Plato and Aristotle. The Romans are studied chiefly for their contributions to Western law and governance. The texts and courses move then to medieval political thought and the Catholic-Christian systems of Augustine and Aquinas. Toward the end of the first semester, several rays of light are often

12

perceived in these otherwise "dark" ages: early glimmerings of the ideas and concepts that will come to undergird the "secular" nation-state, nascent justifications for the separation of church and state, and arguments in favor of limited government.

The big break comes with Machiavelli, either before or just after the midyear vacation. Political scientists tend to like Machiavelli (although not countenancing all he advocates) more than Aquinas, let us say, because he is perceived as the first real modern, a thoroughly rational, secular, pragmatic, and realistic thinker, who coolly analyzes political power and how to achieve and exercise it, presumably without the religious and ethical inhibitions of his predecessors. It is probable that political scientists admire Machiavelli because in these traits he conforms closely to our own notions of ourselves and our discipline. But while admiring Machiavelli, we typically forget the explicit repudiation of his ideas elsewhere in Italy and France, and in the writings of a prolific group of Spanish theorists—Suárez, Molina, Vitoria, and Mariana—who rejected the sharp distinction between politics and ethics and continued to advance theories of a polity based on the credentials of logic, rightness, relation to abstract justice, and the continued integration of the social and the moral.[6] But owing to the prejudices that we as social scientists hold and the way we structure our courses, this important strand in the history of Western thought has been conveniently ignored.

After Machiavelli we turn generally to Hobbes, another purely secular analyst of political power, and then to the basis of liberal-democratic rule in Locke. The Protestant Reformation is similarly viewed positively, on balance, because of its break with Catholic orthodoxy, the pluralism of ideas it helped usher in, and its rationalizations for individual initiative, local self-rule, the rise of capitalism, and democratic choice. Our point here is not to question these as values but to show that they represent one set of values among several and that by our celebratory treatment of them and lack of attention to other traditions, we inevitably prejudice our understanding of the history of Western thought.

Beginning with the eighteenth-century Enlightenment, our typical political theory courses become even more narrowly circumscribed. It is during this period that many of our modern notions of progress, rationality, popular government, and secularism flourish; but these concepts are again based on the experience of a very small, select group of countries and experiences. Our attention focuses on Rousseau, Voltaire, and the French Revolution; Hume, Bentham, Smith, Ricardo, Mill, and perhaps T. H. Green and the development of British liberalism and utilitarianism; and the tradition of German idealism in Kant, Hegel, and eventually Marx. Depending on how far behind we are in our syllabi, we may then present an analysis of the great alternative ideologies of the early twentieth century: socialism with its democratic and Communist variations, liberalism, and fascism—as if these were the only contemporary alternatives available.

Several criticisms may be leveled regarding the organization of this more or less representative political theory course. These concerns seem especially important because there are remarkable parallels in the structuring of our "History of Western Civ" and other courses that form the core of our liberal arts curriculum and because, it seems apparent, these concepts learned in college by generations of students in the 1950s, 1960s, and 1970s have powerfully conditioned our social science understandings, our assumptions about the world, and the policies flowing from them.

First, these courses have an almost exclusively Western focus. From beginning (Greece, Rome, and the Judeo-Christian tradition) to end (the alternative twentieth-century ideologies), it is only the Western and European historical theater of ideas and experiences that receives attention. It is hardly remarkable to point this out, and certainly most who teach these courses would agree this represents a major bias. Nowhere in these courses is there any examination of Taoist, Confucian, Buddhist, Hindu, Islamic, or African ideas, institutions, or concepts of change; worse, there is seldom mention that such exist or that they are worthy of study. One supposes that when we believed, as we once did (and some still do) that development inevitably meant Westernization, that in order for Third World nations to develop and enter the mainstream of history (recall both Hegel and Marx claiming arrogantly and ethnocentrically that the non-Western nations had "no history" or were locked in "pre-history"), they first had to overcome their traditional indigenous institutions and shuck off their historical cultures and beliefs, then such omissions might have been rationalizable.

By this time, we know: (1) development does not, automatically or inevitably, imply or produce Westernization—many forms of modernization are possible (in Japan or the Islamic countries, for example) that do not necessarily mean Westernization; (2) the Western–non-Western or traditional-modern dichotomies are in any case misleading and far too restrictive of the range of possibilities open;[7] (3) traditional beliefs and institutions, rather than being swept aside or superseded as modernization goes forward, have proved to have remarkable staying power, flexibility, and adaptability;[8] and (4) many Third World nations have by now rejected in whole or in part, the models of the already developed world and are searching in their own histories and cultures for indigenous frameworks more in keeping with their own customs and realities.

These changes have left a whole generation and more of social scientists and policy makers at a loss. Their assumptions of universal and inevitable Westernization and modernization no longer wash; yet that is the only model they know since very few have the advanced and specialized training in non-Western frameworks to conceive of development in any other way. Our incomprehension of and the vague (and often not so vague) hostility toward events like the Iranian revolution provide a recent illustration. Whatever our views on Iranian-American relations, on the taking of the American hostages, or of Iran's resort to terrorist techniques, internal events in Iran, particularly the resurrection of an Islamic state and the restoration of many traditional practices and institutions, are often incomprehensible to us both because they do not fit our Western models and because we know virtually nothing regarding Islamic ways and political thought. The absence of more than a handful of persons in the U.S. Department of State, as in academia or the nation at large, who know anything about the Islamic tradition—from an empathetic rather than a hostile viewpoint—not only helps us understand why our foreign policy has been so inadequate but also reflects a broader malaise: our continued belief in the superiority and inevitability of the Western way and our ignorance and disparagement of all others.

Even within the Western tradition, however, our history-of-political-thought courses may be criticized for the selectivity involved in stressing certain ideas and concepts as opposed to others. Once past the feudal period, these courses are highly discriminating in focusing on what are perceived as modernizing ideas or focuses or, conversely, in consigning to obscurity those seen as nonprogressive or traditional. Among the latter, in addition to the Catholic-organic conception already noted, are elitism, social hierarchy, mercantilism, corporatism, familialism and kinship, authoritarianism, ascriptive criteria, patrimonialism, localism, divine right, and so on. Those in the former category include an emphasis on (and implied admiration for) secularism, pluralism, democracy, rationalism, pragmatism, equality, and so forth. These are admirable values, of course, but they also represent political choices or cultural givens, and one may question whether these values ought to be emphasized to the exclusion of all others. Nor should history be presented as if one particular set of desired values is universal, inevitable, and the end point toward which all nations aspire. Even the sharp distinction we draw between traditional and modern is itself a product of our Western historical experience and would not be so sharply drawn in other cultural areas. It seems likely these values and interpretations of history are stressed because they represent what we think of as the Western tradition as well as the political preferences and ideology of the political science profession or some segments of it; and the belief that one's own values are both superior and inevitable is always pleasant. But such an approach is not good history, fails to square with the empirical facts, and renders a disservice to our understanding of numerous alternative currents in both Western and non-Western thought. The fact that many social and political analysts are now reexamining not only their assumption about the Third World but also the biases in the Western tradition itself, and the way it is taught, would seem to be a healthy step in the right direction.

Another criticism, related to the previous, concerns the selectivity used in determining which parts of the West are to be studied. For once in the modern era our attention focuses almost exclusively on three countries—England, France, and Germany—their developmental experiences, and the major intellectual figures who have chronicled or rationalized these changes. Obviously these are important traditions out of which many of us come, but unless one can make the increasingly doubtful argument that the developmental processes of other nations *must* follow the path of these three—especially the paradigmatic cases of the French Revolution of 1789 and the social and political crosscurrents to which it gave rise, or the English experience of industrialization, 1760–1830, and its accompanying effects—the patterns of change in these nations should not be treated as the only or even most advanced model. Left out in such a view are the quite distinct experiences of northern Europe (the Scandinavian countries), eastern Europe, and southern Europe (Greece, Italy, Portugal, and Spain). If one is to speak of a Western model, after all, then it is incumbent that all, or at least most, Western nations, not just a select few, be included.[9]

The social science "out" has been to consider England, France, and Germany as the leaders or "norm" (whatever that means, given their diverse histories), the models others must emulate, and the rest as somehow deviant or less developed. Eventually Scandinavia and the Benelux countries came to approximate the model and were thus deemed acceptable and worthy of study, but eastern Europe and southern Europe still did not. That fact was seldom upsetting to social science theory, however, since if some countries failed to fit the paradigm it was the countries and their social and political systems that were condemned or deemed exceptional, not the paradigm that needed assessment. That plus the fact that the nations of southern Europe, especially, still exhibited many traditional features such as persistent authoritarianism, elitism, and corporatism enabled much social science to continue labeling these nations as retarded or under-developed, perhaps someday capable of catching up with the West once they had rid themselves of these nefarious features. That, after all, is what the Western model had comfortably suggested, that such changes or catching up were inherent in development and inevitable.

Little thought was given to the possibility that the corporatist systems of Spain and Portugal, for instance, might represent an *alternative* route to modernization rather than just backward deviations from the progressive Western (actually, only northwest European) model. Because of our democratic biases and our identification of corporatism with fascism, we remain hostile to the theory of corporatism and its ideological background.[10] Pareto and Mosca also seldom find a place in our political theory courses both because they do not fit our preconceived notions and because we do not like elitist and un-democratic theories, particularly those that are unabashedly so. From this and other factors stem the dislike and incomprehension that both the social sciences and policy makers sometimes harbor toward the southern European nations especially, those "damnable and unsta-ble" (as if the two were synonymous) countries, as Henry Kissinger once put it scornfully, that lie over the Alps or Pyrenees ("beyond the pale of civilization," as Metternich said). Let us not take this argument further for now except to say that it is not just in the non-Western world where the European-based model, ideology, and dominant po-litical beliefs fail to apply, but they may also be only narrowly applica-ble in significant parts of the very European context where the model was born.[11]

To assert that the great Western tradition of political thought with which we are familiar is of less than universal applicability and that there are major geographic and cultural areas, including some within the West, that are entirely neglected in our political and social theory courses is to imply that there *is* something worth studying in these other areas and traditions. That is a difficult proposition to demon-strate to those who have always thought in Eurocentric terms, and it helps explain why so many of those studying other areas spend much of their professional careers defensively seeking to justify to their colleagues why their areas may be just as profound and complex, with as many important research implications, as Britain, France, Ger-many, or the United States. It is a long, uphill battle, which is still only partially won but seems to be gaining added momentum due to the growing malaise within these core areas in recent years and the cor-responding increase in importance of such previously neglected na-tions as Brazil, China, India, Iran, Mexico, Nigeria, and Tanzania.

17

In my own research and writing I have tried to show the continued importance of Iberian and Latin American organic-corporatist thought and sociopolitical organization, to present this as a viable alternative to the usual liberal-pluralist models with which we look at these areas and to understand Latin America, in the words of novelist Carlos Fuentes, as a distinct *civilization* and not as a series of agreements about tomatoes (or coffee, sugar, or bananas). In other quite distinct cultural and national settings, comparable studies are now appearing or being rediscovered of traditions of thought, law, and social and political organization that were previously ignored and remain largely unknown but that are probably at least as important as the European ones for analyzing these nations' unique developmental processes. It is not our purpose here to describe these alternative traditions in any detail but merely to note that they exist and to point readers toward some of the literature.[12]

Political Sociology. Political sociology demonstrates many of the same biases as does political theory and is probably more dangerous because sociology is taken more seriously than political theory. Indeed, an entire generation and more grew up with the development sociology literature of the past three decades, a body of literature that is as narrow, particularistic, ethnocentric, and Western-biased as the theory just analyzed.

Since Durkheim, sociologists have generally assumed that the processes of modernization are more-or-less universal. Once industrialization begins, a number of concomitant changes occur in the structure of society, class organization, social mobility, behavior patterns, division of labor, and the like. These alterations occur regardless of cultural context: indeed, their very power as motor forces of change tends to erase cultural, linguistic, or geographic differences.[13]

It is not our purpose here to offer a detailed critique of Durkheim's seminal work or of Marx's analysis of the social and political effects of industrialization, on which so much of modern sociology is based. We grant the general utility of some of these conceptions at the level of broad abstraction and as heuristic devices. It is our contention, however, that these are starting points of explanation, not end points, necessary explanations but not sufficient ones. Durkheim (Marx is treated later) was, of course, a European writing of a particular time and place, a philosopher of the French university, a spiritual descendant of Auguste Comte and the Enlightenment, and a believer in social consensus and progress, shaped by both the intellectual climate of France at the end of the nineteenth century and by the social changes then under way in Paris.[14] He had little knowledge of events and cultures outside Europe, and his research dealt chiefly with the Western European (actually French) concomitants of economic growth. Obviously, the conditions of the present-day emerging nations, the timing and sequences of their development, and the international context are quite different from that of the European countries a century ago. With our more extensive research in non-Western areas we now know how distinct cultural contexts and institutions can filter, screen out, and mediate if not determine the social and political effects of industrialization. Moreover, while Durkheim limited himself to outlining only some of the broad and general societal concomitants of industrialization (increased specialization and the division of labor may well be universal, for instance), latter-day sociologists went considerably beyond his findings to identify very specific changes in political party organization, governmental organization, trade union and military behavior, and the like, as also following necessarily from modernization. It is at this level of quite specific indicators and predictors of the sociopolitical concomitants of modernization, again and inexcusably all derived from the Euro-American experience, that ideal types became confused with reality and the biases and ethnocentrism of political sociology became most apparent.

The empirical evidence does not support the claims to universalism and inevitability put forth by the major Western theories of sociopolitical development concerning the impact of industrialization on the broader social system.[15] The transition from an agrarian society to an industrial one and such factors as increased population, urbanization, the separation of place of residence from place of work, coupled with rising occupational differentiation and specialization have tended *in the West* to have brought specific kinds of changes in familial, religious, political, and all other major areas of social organization. It is for this reason, and because at that time the sociologists and political economists who analyzed these changes were themselves exclusively from that area, that the specifically Western social and political concomitants of industrialization came to be incorporated into theoretical conceptualizations of the change process per se. Given the historical context (the mid-to-late nineteenth century) and the fact that northwest Europe experienced these mammoth changes first (and particularly at that time the lack of any non-Western experience with the transition to an industrial society), one might well say that the Western social adaptations occurring then almost *had* to be closely associated with a more general and presumptively universal theory of development and modernization.

The Western bias pervades the work of the great figures in sociology. For example, Weber's and Tawney's work on the mutual influence of religion and economics in the growth of rational capitalism, Toennies's *Gemeinschaft* and *Gesellschaft*, Durkheim's mechanical and organic solidarity, and the mass society concept developed by MacIver are major examples of analyses concerned with particular aspects of a particular *Western* cultural history. The development literature was largely grounded on this same set of concepts and understandings, generalizing unduly from what was a narrow and limited historical and cultural experience. There is no reason to assume that in other cultural areas the same sociopolitical concomitants of industrialization must necessarily follow. Students of non-Western or partly Western areas, whose development is taking place in a quite different context, must face the more difficult task of distinguishing between the processes and dynamics of industrialization *and* the social and political changes accompanying these that may take quite different and varied directions from those of the West.

Not only are the timing, sequences, and international context of development different, but non-Western societies have generally been quite selective in accepting what is useful from Western modernization while often rejecting the rest. Of course, this is a mixed situation, for while some elements associated with Western modernization are kept out, other aspects enter regardless of the barriers erected. But the process itself is one of filtering and not simply of imitating and inevitably following. Japanese modernization under the Meiji, for example, came about through the cooperation of government and powerful family groups. The tenacity of such traditional family elements and their persistence were not the result merely of nostalgic attachment to the past or to some vague tradition; rather there were valid economic reasons—Japan's abundance of manpower as opposed to capital, her traditional family handicraft industry that could be used to generate the needed capital—for their retention. As a result, the Japanese pattern of modernization has indicated significant differences from that of the West (and it obviously continues to do so). The social and political concomitants that in the West followed from industrialization have not necessarily followed.

The Japanese evidence and parallel findings from other regions of the world suggest that the forms of Western social and political organization are not the inevitable consequence of the replacement of feudalism, traditionalism, and agriculturalism by a modern industrial technology. Instead, the capitalistic individualism, secularism, the particular role of the middle classes and middle "classness," the growth of liberalism and interest group pluralism, and a host of other features that are so much a part of the northwest European and U.S.

religious, familial, social, and political system should be seen as only one of numerous possible alternatives in the urban-industrial transition, and not necessarily a more developed or ethically or morally superior one. Other, *alternative* routes to modernization also command our attention.

Modern political sociology and the development literature derived in large measure from the perspectives outlined above and from the "pattern variables" of Talcott Parsons.[16] Parsons advanced three (occasionally four) measures to gauge the transition from traditional to modern, whether in society, polity, or even individual personality. Thus, whereas traditional society is functionally "diffuse," modern society is functionally "specific"; whereas traditional society is "particularistic," modern society is "universalistic"; whereas traditional society is based on "ascription," modern society is based on "achievement." In the works of such prominent scholars as Sutton, Shils, Deutsch, Lerner, Riggs, Lipset, Almond, Levy, and Black, who wrote on developmental themes, these pattern variables became a key means to distinguish between traditional and modern, underdeveloped and developed. The industrialized, modern, and developed society is thus characterized by law, regular procedures, merit, and the like, while the agrarian, traditional, underdeveloped society is characterized by custom, status, ascription, and the like.[17] The Western model's relevance in explaining the transition from the latter to the former was assumed to be global. Armed with the "certainties" this assumption and the pattern variables provided, waves of graduate students and well-meaning Peace Corpsmen and AID staffers fanned out to the Third World to find development and advance it.

The importance of these categories and the impact of the development literature derived from it cannot be overemphasized. The Parsonian schema provided a common set of concepts and theory and a means to help unify the social sciences that had not existed for a long time before—or since. The development literature provided the basis for thousands of doctoral dissertations in anthropology, economics, political science, and sociology, which took the theory and applied it to a host of old and new countries in Africa, Asia, Latin America, and the Middle East. It was also the basis of the Alliance for Progress and the U.S. foreign aid programs, positing à la Lipset or W. W. Rostow, that if only enough money were poured in and economic growth stimulated, a middle class would grow, labor and peasants would become less radical, society and polity would become more pluralist and just, the armed forces would become more professionalized and stay out of politics, the appeals of communism would diminish, and so on. The same sequences of development that occurred in

21

the West must also occur elsewhere. The developing nations would thus modernize and in the process come to look just like us. What we think of as the great names in the profession largely earned their status by writing on such developmental themes, and both the dominant literature and almost all our understanding of how societies grow, modernize, democratize, etc., derive from this common set of assumptions. One of the more interesting aspects of this phenomenon, and a measure of the dominance of the Western-oriented development theory, is the degree to which social scientists in the Third World—at least for a time—also absorbed these intellectual constructs.

The problems with the pattern variable and Western-oriented developmental approach are numerous. In the first place the pattern variables imply a sharp dualism that in actual fact does not exist. The sharpness of the breaks ushered in with the English, French, and Russian revolutions lent support to this view, but it was not relevant to most non-Western areas. The more sophisticated developmentalists recognized that the pattern variables represented continua, not either-or situations and that most societies consisted of diverse mixes and fusions of traditional and modern, and further that these were ideal types, heuristic devices, or shorthand terms with no necessary correlation with reality. However, many forgot this distinction, confused approximations of reality with the real things, became so used to the shorthand that it came to have real substance, even reified these artificial concepts and applied them to actual, existing institutions. One of the most dangerous tendencies was to treat the developing countries not only as less developed economically and sociopolitically but psychologically and morally as well. More often implicitly than explicitly, underdeveloped countries became underdeveloped peoples, and the implications of that are so scary, condescending, and obvious that the argument need not be detained by further details.

In sociology as in political theory, the models and metaphors used derived exclusively from the Euro-American experience. It is not necessary here to go into non-Western concepts of time and space, cyclical theories of history as opposed to the predominantly evolutionary ones of the West, or notions of permanence and continuity as opposed to Western belief in perpetual change. Suffice it to say that the images used to depict development were all Western in origin and that we had no comprehension of societies based on presumptions other than that of constant progress. How arrogant that no consideration was given to non-Western concepts, except as these constituted traditional, dysfunctional "problems to be overcome!" It is small wonder that theories purporting to be universal but actually quite particularistic should run up against major barriers or produce unexpected results when they were applied to societies where their major assumptions had no bases in local history, tradition, or understandings.

Especially presumptuous was the expectation of a single, unilinear path to development. There was only one acceptable route along with certain common signposts—all derived from the Western experience—along the path. Traditional society was seldom further differentiated, leaving the impression that all Third World nations had evolved from a common background and had begun at the same starting point; and, once started, they had embarked on a single path that led them to shed their traditional features and proceed irreversibly to modernization. Almost no thought was given to the fact that not only were the starting points and the natures of traditional societies immensely different, but that the paths to development and the end products were certain to be vastly dissimilar as well. The image that should have been used was not that of a single path or route to development but that of a much more complex *lattice*, with numerous, diverse beginnings and multiple, crisscrossing channels.[18]

A key reason developmental sociology went astray—and a major cause of its attractiveness—is that a close identification was made between development as a process and development as a moral and ethical good. As social scientists we could analyze development and identify with it as well; like apple pie and motherhood, development was seen as a desirable normative goal toward which all "right-thinking" people should surely work. Particularly as development was closely identified with the values that social scientists hold—secularism, rationalism, pluralism, and the like—and as it implied the destruction or replacement of the values and institutions social scientists tend not to like (authoritarian and traditional structures; religious beliefs and institutions; familial, tribal, or clan ties), it carried enormous appeal.

There is certainly something we can analyze as *change*; "development" and "modernization" are probably too Western, too loaded, to be of much use in describing Third World events. But change should be regarded as a neutral process and not involve the intrusion of ethical, political, or moral judgments—unless we are willing to abandon all pretense to objectivity and assume that our private values are or ought to be everyone's values. That is highly conceited and pretentious. Certainly it is difficult to be against development and modernization. The mistake was that social science presumed to *know* what a developed society looked like (liberal, pluralist, democratic: our idealized image of ourselves) and that it assumed that the values of Western civilization were or had to become everyone's values. Hence, if traditional societies or institutions—African tribalism, Indian caste as-

23

sociations, a host of others—failed to develop in terms of prevailing social science theory, they had of necessity to be uprooted and obliterated in favor of new modernizing ones; and if in the process the modernizing institutions such as political parties and trade unions failed to develop, it was again the societies that were dysfunctional rather than the theory that needed reexamination.

Seen as an ethical good in accord with narrow Euro-American perceptions, development also closely served U.S. foreign policy goals. One treads cautiously here to avoid engaging in verbal overkill or to make the ludicrous claims that some fringe-radical critics of U.S. policy have. One need not be on the fringes to recognize that the development literature and strategies served as a convenient means to expand immensely the U.S. presence in the developing world. Development helped rationalize the large number of labor officials, tax specialists, agrarian reform technicians, businessmen, AID administrators, academic experts of all sorts, Peace Corpsmen, and others sent abroad during the heyday of both U.S. power and concern for development. The sheer amounts of money and U.S. personnel involved converted many smaller and weaker Third World nations into quasi-dependencies of the United States—whether that was part of a conscious design or no. The effort to bring development to the Third World succeeded in pulling many of these nations into the U.S. orbit, increasing our influence and levers of manipulation there, making them dependent on us, imposing our preferred solutions on them, and thus strengthening our hand in a global cold war struggle. It is precisely the nationalistic reaction against these influences, against American economic, cultural, military and political domination that we are now reaping in Latin America and throughout the globe.

Such nationalistic or cultural-area (as in the Islamic world) reactions against the Euro-American development model make it doubly ironic that the bulk of the literature saw such development both as an ethical good and as an inevitable process. Ultimately all societies, it was argued, had to go through the same or similar modernization. It is of course enormously comforting to social scientists to know that what they are studying is not only scientific, ethically good, and supportive of the national interest, but also inevitable. Development studies had strong elements of both moral self-righteousness and absolute certainty, while also serving our foreign policy objectives. We were comfortable in knowing that what we studied and advocated was morally just and that in the long run, despite occasional coups, revolutions, and other dysfunctional reversals, our developmental formulas were bound to be correct and that the emerging nations would ultimately conform to our preferred model.

24

There are, certainly, universals in the development process, and perhaps Western Europe and the United States provide us with a model of how this occurs. Economic development and industrialization *are* occurring in virtually all areas of the globe; class transformations are under way; people are being uprooted and mobilized; urbanization is accelerating; traditional institutions are changing and new ones are being created; specialization and differentiation are going forward. The mistake of the development literature was in ascribing specific social and political concomitants to these changes based on a model that was not universalistic, as it claimed, but particularistic and narrowly Euro-American. Because all economic and class transformations are, after all, filtered through and shaped by distinct, indigenous cultural, social, and political institutions, no less so in the Third World than in Western Europe, the timing, sequences, and context of these changes are also quite varied. What the social sciences did, however, was to generalize inappropriately from the sociopolitical institutional concomitants of modernization in Western Europe, which they knew best and assumed to be desirable, to other nations, which they knew less well and with whose traditional institutions they felt uncomfortable. Generalization from a single unique case to the rest of the world is not unusual among social scientists; in the case of the development literature, however, the assumptions were widely shared, and the results for developing nations have often been particularly unfortunate. The costs of this myopia we have recently begun to pay.

Political Economy. Economics as a discipline is, along with sociology, most explicit in its claims to universality. Therein lies one of the world's great problems.

Two grand traditions exist in economic thought: the Marxian and the non-Marxian. Both are based on the Western European experience. Neither, in their classical forms, or taken without qualification or without appending major amendments, is of great utility in dealing with the realities of the non-Euro-American world.

What Marx had to say about the non-Western or Asiatic nations, disparaging their cultures and condemning them to prehistory, was not very flattering;[19] but that is not our chief concern here. What does concern us is the selective use of history by Marx to argue his famous case, and the oftentimes mindless and unqualified application by his latter-day disciples of his major categories to societies where they fit but imperfectly and incompletely. It is common knowledge that the national sources for Marx's philosophic and empirical work were mainly three: philosophically it was German thought and idealism

25

that strongly shaped his concepts; he took most of his political illustrations from French history; and his understanding of industrialization and its effects was principally derived from the English experience. Certainly no one would deny the importance of these histories or of Marx's influence. The questions center on the small size of the sample, its representativeness, whether the experiences of these three early modernizers are relevant to the situation of Third World nations today, and whether the mid-nineteenth-century European context may not have been so unique as to carry but limited lessons for the non-Western world. Marx himself, after all, consistently cautioned his followers that his analysis derived from and was meant to apply to Western Europe.

Economic and class changes are obviously occurring also in the Third World, but we make a mistake if we think that social and political institutions in these nations are or will be the exact mirror of underlying class structure—or that they will everywhere be the same. Nor is it the case that political forces in these societies can always be subordinated to economic variables; rather, the reverse process often occurs, with class structure and economic change shaped by cultural, social, or political institutions. Nor is it accurate or even realistic to expect that the experience of a highly select group of countries in the nineteenth century will be repeated in exact or even similar form in the developing nations today. One must question whether England really provides *the* paradigm case of the capitalistic mode of production. Nor can we assume as Marx did that the same organization of production will necessarily generate the same class and political changes, the same developmental epochs or typical sequences. Nor should we think that the social and political changes that accompanied these transformations in northwest Europe will inevitably reappear in non-Western areas in parallel form. The international contexts of dependence and interdependence are so different, the cultural and institutional milieu so varied, and the social and political filters governing the way these changes take place or are perceived are so distinctive that it is preposterous to think that the developing nations will repeat, albeit much later, the experiences of economic development of Western Europe or the United States.

Non-Marxian developmental economics is as Eurocentric as the classical Marxian variety. The famous aeronautical stages in the "non-Communist manifesto" of W. W. Rostow ("drive to take off," "take off," etc.), which so strongly shaped—as did Parsons and Lipset in sociology and the Almond and Coleman volume on "The Politics of the Developing Nations" in political science—whole generations of development-minded economists, were based almost exclusively on

26

the Western European and U.S. experiences. The logic of the Rostow analysis (and of the Alliance for Progress and U.S. foreign assistance, since as Chair of Policy Planning at the State Department and then as National Security Adviser Rostow was also the chief influence in shaping these programs) was that if only the United States could pour in sufficient economic aid, "take off" would occur and the following social and political effects would be felt: organized labor would become less extremist and revolutionary; more professional, and hence less political, armies and bureaucracies would grow; a large middle class would emerge as a bulwark of stable, middle-of-the-road rule; the peasants would become yeomen, middle-class family farmers; and radical ideologies such as communism and fascism would diminish in attractiveness.

These assumptions, originating in the literature on European and U.S. economic history (Japan fit uncomfortably in Rostow's analysis) undergirded both much social science theory and the U.S. foreign aid program during the 1960s and 1970s. It was an application of the Marshall Plan, successful in Western European *recovery*, to Third World nations where the cultural conditions and economic and political givens were fundamentally different. The assumption was that if we provided economic aid, sent our technical experts, promoted agrarian reform, trained the local army, reformed the tax system, encouraged local community development, pushed family planning, provided for administrative reform, and all the other developmental panaceas that have had their own life histories during the past two decades,[20] modernization would certainly take place and these "aspiring nations" could be recast in our own image.

Large numbers of developmentally trained academics were enlisted during this period to assist the U.S. government and a host of quasi-public, though ostensibly private, foundations and other agencies with this effort to bring modernization to less-favored lands. Even the language was reminiscent of the missionary's patronizing zeal to *bring* Christianity to "our little brown and black brothers." Literally thousands of social scientists (I was no exception) flew off to Africa, Asia, Latin America, and the Middle East to put their technical expertise to work. Few questioned the assumptions of the Western-derived developmentalist model, and not just because travel expenses and an honorarium were involved. We really believed our models were universally relevant. If difficulties arose, whole programs wasted, or unanticipated consequences produced, these were consistently viewed as problems to be overcome or dysfunctional aspects that could be solved by more aid and technical expertise. Little consideration was afforded the idea that indigenous social and political institutions

27

might represent the givens to work with rather than merely problems to be overcome. If a particular program misfired (there are some spectacular cases) or had little or no effect (the less-spectacular fate of most of the U.S.-conceived programs), it was the Third World country that required reform, seldom the program itself.

Less sanguine observers of these programs were often amazed that the experts really expected a land-reform program appropriate for Wisconsin to work in Peru, a system of local government modeled on the New England town meeting to take root in the centralized code-law nations of Latin America, or a progressive income tax as in the United States to be applied where the expectations regarding the fairness and impartiality of the state were quite different. Watching with wonder as program after program failed or produced meager results and yet where the major assumptions still went unexamined, one came to question if the social scientists and AID administrators were so naive as to believe that they really could work, so unimaginative as to see no other solutions besides the Western ones, or if they continued to push these programs simply because that was their job. Perhaps they did not want to rock the boat or become a naysayer of programs that enjoyed such wide consensus and came wrapped in the mantle of academic social science. Perhaps no one was willing to say that the developmentalist emperor had on no clothes. Doubtless, all these explanations have some validity.

By this point it should be abundantly clear that the Rostowian stages do not necessarily follow one another, that there is no unilinear and inevitable path to development, that with the oil crisis, the internationalization of capital, and other features, the condition of the Third World nations today is fundamentally different from those prevailing a century or more ago, that the development process in these nations hence will not and cannot be a mirror of the European experience, that there are numerous culturally conditioned routes to modernization and not just the European one, and therefore that the social and political concomitants which, based on the European experience, are supposed to follow from modernization may not, in these quite different temporal and spatial contexts, follow at all.[21] Rather, development will take directions that reflect indigenous traditions and institutions; and it is time that we recognize this fact rather than continue to dismiss these processes and institutions as dysfunctional or try to interpret them through a Western social science framework that has only limited relevance in non-Western areas. As David Apter reminded us some time ago, industrialization in the West is only one form of industrialization.[22] The dilemma for most developing nations is hence not Westernization or even modernization but how to gain and employ Western capital and technology while preserving what they see as valuable in their own cultures and traditions.

Consequences of the Western Biases

The northwest European and North American biases on which so much of our political theory, sociology, and economics are based have produced major consequences, many of them unfortunate so far as a better comprehension of the developing nations goes. Our ethnocentrism has led not just to continued misinterpretation, however, but also to immense and often negative practical consequences for these nations. In this realm the ideas of academics and policy makers *have* had an impact, unfortunate though that has frequently been. After all, social scientists and policy makers generally spend at best a year or two in their countries of specialization and can fly off at any time when their theories or programs prove wrong; left behind, however, are the people of the developing nation who have no choice but to try to cope as best they can with the misfortunes wrought upon them. We propose here to examine briefly only a few of the results of our social science biases, under three categories: those subject matters to which we have unwarrantedly given too much attention, those we have afforded too little, and the damage we have wreaked upon the developing nations because of our ethnocentrism.

The theory and assumptions we have applied to the developing nations have often led us to expect certain trends to occur and institutions to develop that have, in fact, not consistently developed. We have expected, and perhaps hoped, that modernization would produce more pluralist and secular societies when, in fact, in Iran and elsewhere powerful religious revivals are taking place that are monistic and theocratic and that proclaim a single right-and-wrong way to do everything, which seems appallingly oppressive to most Westerners. We celebrate democracy and pluralism in our theories in the political sphere as well, when the real question in virtually all developing nations is which form authoritarianism will take.[23] We have expected more universalist criteria to take hold when in fact particularism seems everywhere on the rise. We applaud merit and have elevated it to a universal norm of modernity when the fact is ascriptive criteria seem ascendant, perhaps increasingly so even in our own society. Obviously, differentiation of labor, specialization of function, and rationalization and bureaucratization have occurred throughout the developing world, but rather than producing much democratization in countries where a strong imperious central state has been either the norm or the aspiration, these trends have chiefly produced

29

more efficient and centralized forms of statism and even terror.[24]

Our social science assumptions have also led us to look for the growth of an increasingly more prosperous working class and hence a more apolitical trade unionism, when in fact, in Brazil, Argentina, and elsewhere the latter does not seem necessarily to follow from the former. We expected an increasingly professional and thus apolitical military, when in fact increased professionalism leads many militaries (Brazil, Egypt, Indonesia, Peru, Portugal) to become more political rather than less. We hoped for stronger local government, when in fact the dominant tendency even of our community development programs has been toward greater concentration of state power. We predicted mass-based political parties that would perform the interest aggregation and articulation functions when actually most parties in the developing nations are that only in name and may not at all be inclined to perform the functions Western political science assigns to them. We believed that the middle class would be moderate, democratic, and inclined to assist the less-favored elements in the society, when in fact the divided middle sectors in most Third World nations are inclined to ape upper-class ways and use the instruments of the state (armies, labor ministries, and the like) to keep their own lower classes subservient. We expected elites and businessmen to recognize their social responsibilities to the poor in a more pluralist setting, when the real situation is that the elites are intent not on sharing but on getting more wealth and monopolizing it. We thought that greater respect for civil liberties and democracy would evolve, rather than the increased statism, authoritarianism, and corporatism that seem to be the real-life situation virtually everywhere in the Third World. The list of misapplied theories and programs goes on and on. In short, few of the social and political concomitants of modernization that our Western experience would lead us to expect to see developing are in fact developing. The problem lies not in the developing areas since they are often merely continuing preferred and traditional practices; rather, the problem lies in the Western-based concepts and often wishful social science with which we have sought to interpret these nations.

At the same time that too much attention has been devoted to those institutions that, based on the Western experience, social scientists expected or hoped to develop, too little has been afforded those not in accord with these preferences. It seems obvious, for example, that in the Islamic world and elsewhere religious beliefs and institutions cannot simply be relegated to the ashcans of history under the "inevitable" onslaught of secularism, nor can the former be dismissed as part of traditional society certain to be superseded. The same applies to tribal and caste associations: these are not just traditional institutions certain to give way under modernization's impact. Behind much of the ideological skirmishing in Africa, for instance, is a tribal context, one that should not be denied or wished away as much social science does but taken as a given and perhaps as a base for social and political associations other than the preferred Western ones. Similarly, India's caste associations are now viewed as adaptable institutions capable of serving as modernizing agencies.[25] There is a refreshing degree of realism now on the part of political leaders and intellectuals in the Third World to take such institutions as givens and potential developmental building blocks rather than as symbols of backwardness that had to be destroyed. The functioning and changes in such institutions during epochs of transition ought also to be a primary focus of social scientists and should not be easily dismissed.

With the strong social-democratic bias that undergirds much of the development literature, social scientists have disregarded a variety of other institutions either because we do not like them politically or because they do not fit our preferred models. Most social scientists, for instance, are uncomfortable with, and often quite hostile toward, the Catholic, elitist, and authoritarian assumptions of traditional Latin society. Because we do not like elite-structured societies, we have seldom studied the dynamics of elite strategies and elite networks, preferring to dismiss these out of hand or apply the familiar traditional label, which seemingly helps make the problem go away. There is abundant literature on labor and peasant movements but very little on elites, both because of practical research problems and because social scientists, like most Americans, are ill at ease with elitist assumptions. We do not like theocratic societies either and especially despise the Islamic mullahs for seeking to resurrect one, but our understanding of events in Iran and other nations will not be advanced by complete hostility or the dismissal of such popular movements as irrational.

Military coups provide another illustration of the familiar biases. Most Western social science, with its favoritism toward democratic and civilian government, treats coups as aberrations—irregular, dysfunctional, and unconstitutional—thus ignoring their normality, regularity, workability, often legal-constitutional basis, the reasons for them, their functional similarity to elections, and the fact the former may be no more comic opera than the latter. Our antimilitary bias, however, often prevents us from seeing these events neutrally and scientifically.[26]

The examples of such ethnocentrism are numerous in the areas of both public policy and institutions. In President Carter's human rights campaign, for example, it was consistently the U.S. model and

31

understanding that were imposed abroad; no consideration was given to the fact that other societies define terms like "rights," "democracy," or "justice" in different ways, that they see these differently or assign them a different priority.[27] One pales also at the thought of how many countries and how many women and men in them have been called irrational because they desire larger families rather than smaller, a decision that in their individual circumstances may well be perfectly rational. Or, in another tradition, one wonders at the easy and widespread use of the term "false consciousness" to describe peasants and workers who may be uncomfortable with or suspicious of revolutionary movements organized, so they claim, on the lower classes' behalf.[28] The number of policy areas and institutions in which labels and slogans substitute for close examination, or where dismissal to the dustbins of history or to the ranks of traditionalism or dysfunctionality substitutes for hard analysis, seems almost endless. Even whole continents and regions, such as Latin America and Africa, are often dismissed by social scientists as areas without political culture and therefore unworthy of study. Such attitudes reflect not the true importance of these areas but the biases of the social sciences; for these areas seldom fit our favored models, and we are often vaguely antipathetic toward their underlying premises.[29]

If these errors of both commission and omission by social scientists and policy makers were merely benignly neutral, there would be little to worry about. Unfortunately, such errors and oversights are not benign, neutral, or harmless. The subject merits much fuller attention; here let it simply be said that (1) based on the ethnocentric developmental assumptions of the social sciences, enormous amounts of money and effort have been wasted on a variety of misguided and misdirected programs; (2) confirmed in the modernity and hence superiority of our own institutions, we have continued patronizingly to dismiss or disparage as traditional or primitive a large number of beliefs, practices, and institutions in the Third World; (3) because our models and perspectives are so narrow and Eurocentric, our comprehension of the real dynamics of change and continuity in these nations remains woefully inadequate, based more on prejudice or romance than on actuality; (4) grounded on this same particularistic and ethnocentric northwest European and U.S. experience, the policy measures we have sought to implement have produced hosts of backfires, unanticipated consequences, and sheer disasters; and (5) in the name of advancing modernity, we have helped undermine a great variety of quite viable traditional and transitional institutions, thus contributing by our policies to the breakdown, fragmentation, and instability of many developing nations that we had ostensibly sought to avoid.

All these charges are serious, but the last one may have the gravest long-term consequences. By helping destroy their traditional institutions and by erecting ephemeral modern ones cast in our own image to replace them but often entirely inappropriate in the societies where we have sought to locate them, we have left many developing nations neither with the traditional and indigenous institutions that might have helped them bridge the wrenching transition to modernity nor with viable new ones that have any basis or hope of functioning effectively in the native soil. By forcing some wrong and falsely dichotomous choices on the developing nations (traditional *or* modern democracy *or* dictatorship), social scientists and policy makers have contributed strongly to the institutional vacuum that plagues these countries and to the hopeless cases that, in the absence of genuinely homegrown institutions, some of them are certain to become.[30]

Conclusions and Implications

The development literature, whether in political science, sociology, or economics, assumes that the path to modernization in the Third World can be explained by reference to the past or the present of the already industrialized nations. Development in Africa, Asia, Latin America, and the Middle East is seen, in Glaucio Ary Dillon Soares's words, as specific instances of a general course of events already studied and fully comprehended in the experience of the Western European countries and the United States.[31] Such an approach assumes that quite distinct cultural areas and historical epochs can be understood using the same terms and concepts as in the West. It assumes a single unilinear path to development and also the universality of what is a far narrower and particular European or Western experience and set of institutions. The ethnocentrism of this interpretation and the absurdity of reducing a great variety of histories and sociopolitical formations to the single matrix of the Western European-U.S. experience are patent. This approach has stultified the creation of new concepts and prevented us from understanding the realities of the developing nations. It has wreaked positive harm upon them and cast the developing nations and those who study them in an inferior position vis-à-vis both the developed countries and those who study them.

A growing chorus of voices in recent years has asked why the United States fails to comprehend and hence anticipate the profound, revolutionary, and anti-American changes sweeping the developing world and why our policy response to these changes has been and remains so inadequate. The Iranian revolution posed most dramatically the questions of why we did not see these occurrences coming, why our policy makers failed to foresee the consequences of their actions, why there are so few scholars or policy makers who have a thorough understanding of Islamic law, institutions, and social change so that we might comprehend Iranian events properly. Iran is not the sole country where such changes are, or are about to be, happening, however; in many Third World countries similar revolutionary winds are blowing. This essay hints at answers to some of the questions posed above.

The problem is that we neither understand nor *want* to understand movements that run counter to the Western conception of change. We *really believe* in both the inevitability and the universality of the Western conception of how change, properly, should go forward. The Eurocentric ideas that we as social scientists and policy makers carry around in our heads and that we studied in college, where we learned all those Parsonian, Rostowian, Almondian, and Lipsetian theories of development, are still the concepts on which our assumptions regarding modernization and development in the Third World are based. The generations grounded so strongly in this tradition are now precisely the generations that are governing us—those in their thirties, forties, and fifties who went to college during the heyday of the developmentalist concepts.

The higher one goes in government, moreover, and hence the more generalists one finds (the president and his advisers, the secretaries and undersecretaries of state and defense, national security advisers, and CIA directors, etc.), the less the expertise on particular nations and cultures is brought to bear, and hence the more policy makers tend, usually only half-consciously, to fall back on the simplistic, narrow, Western, Eurocentric conceptions inculcated in earlier years. How many of these leaders have spent the years outside this country that are required to comprehend fully foreign cultures and institutions? The answer is very few. Indeed, it is in the nature of the American system of politics and career advancement that those spending too long abroad are thought odd and are punished in terms of their possibilities for professional and political advancement at the highest levels. A partial reason why we failed so utterly to comprehend Iranian events, as well as those posed less dramatically for now in scores of other nations, is that our biases and prejudices prevent us from doing so. In fact, our entire educational, socialization, and career system, so heavily European- and U.S.-based, is weighted toward demeaning and denigrating the values and institutions of cultural areas other than our own.

The universals in the modernization process include economic growth and industrialization, class and societal changes, division of labor and increased specialization of functions, rationalization and bureaucratization of society and polity, and the impact of what Lucian Pye once called the "world culture" (not just jeans, Coke, and rock but also outside political ideologies and forces).[32] The difficulty is that the presumed more specific social and political concomitants of these changes—modern political parties, armies, and the like—have not in fact developed simultaneously. The problem is not just "lag" or "uneven development" but that we have failed to appreciate sufficiently the present era's changed circumstances and also the strength and workability of many traditional institutions and how these may shape, mold, and even determine the impact of these larger, more universal changes. We have dismissed as traditional the role of tribes, caste associations, mullahs, religious and fundamentalist movements, elites and family structures, patron-client systems transferred to the national level, and a host of other local and particularistic institutions, rather than seeing them as persistent, flexible, perhaps viable structures on which an indigenous process of development might be based. By now it is clear such institutions will not necessarily disappear or be superseded as modernization proceeds, nor should they be easily dismissed, as our social science literature is wont to do, as dysfunctional. We must recognize the diversity of societies and developmental experiences.

Social scientists must begin with a renewed awareness of their biases, societal likes and dislikes, the Eurocentric basis of so many of their theories, and their particularistic rather than universalistic nature. This will require a fundamental reexamination of most of the truths social scientists, especially North American social scientists, hold to be self-evident. It will also require a new and stronger dose of cultural relativism. Cultural relativism need not be carried so far as to accept or remain neutral toward a Hitler or a Bokassa. But it does imply a much more empathetic understanding of foreign cultures and institutions than before, an understanding of them in terms of their own cultural traditions and even language, rather than through the distorting, blinding prism of Western social science.[33] The social sciences have been guilty of too-hasty generalization; hence, we require more modesty than before concerning the universal applicability of our social science notions, greater uncertainty in our assertions of global social science wisdom, more reluctance to apply the social science findings (apples) of our culture to the realities (oranges) of another, where they neither fit nor add up.[34]

To say that much social science theory we took as universal is somewhat less than that implies that future theory ought probably to be formulated at a lower, cultural-area level. We shall probably have to develop an African social science, an Islamic social science, a Latin American social science, and so on.[35] It may be that such middle-range theory at the cultural-area level will eventually yield again some more general, even universal findings about the development process. This will be a long-term process, however, and we may well find few universals on which to hang our social science hats. Many social scientists will be uncomfortable with this fact; a more useful approach may be to take the absence of very many such universals as a given and proceed from there. Some prominent social scientists are already saying that theory and research at the cultural-area level, the examination of more particularistic, culturally unique, perhaps regionally specific institutions and processes, will probably be the focus of future comparative development studies.[36]

The necessity of analyzing indigenous institutions on their own terms and in their own cultural contexts rather than through Western social science frameworks seems particularly appropriate in the present circumstances, given both the assertion of indigenous ideologies and movements in many development nations and the corresponding rejection of European, American, and Western ones. In my own particular areas of special research interest, for example, Latin America and southern Europe, I have been fascinated both by the new literature on corporatism, dependency, patron-client relations, center-periphery relations, organic-statism, and the like, which have helped form the basis for a new Latin American, or perhaps Iberic-Latin, social science, *and* by the way these concepts have now found their way into interpretations of other areas and into the general literature. It may be that the flow of ideas and concepts, historically from Europe and European studies out to the periphery, may be in the process of being reversed. It may be that Western social scientists will now have to learn from Africa, Asia, Latin America, and the Middle East instead of their always learning from us.[37]

The emergence and articulation of such distinctive Latin American, African, Islamic, and other cultural-area-based sociologies and political sciences of development raise a host of intriguing issues for scholarship. Implied is that we now take the developing nations and their alternative civilizations seriously for the first time, and on their own terms rather than through the condescension and superiority of U.S. or Western European perspectives. It means that the rising sense of nationalism and independence throughout the Third World is likely also to be reflected in a new insistence on indigenous models and institutions of development. It requires the formulation or reformulation of a host of new concepts and interpretations. It also implies that if the West, particularly the United States, can no longer be the world's policeman, it must also exercise restraint in seeking to be its philosopher-king, in terms of its assertion of the universality of its particular developmental experience.

This essay has been something of a broadside. Its claims and criticisms are sweeping. Essentially it says the social sciences of development must start all over. Of course, one purposely overstates the case to make it more forcefully. We have seen that there are universals in the development process, and we need to sort out more carefully what non-Western developing societies allow in and what gets winnowed out. We need sharper distinctions in the present critique between cultural definitions of concepts that implicitly influence social science theory construction, ethnocentrism as a distortion of perception, lack of research in specific culture areas, and simply analogy to the Western development experience, instead of analysis of the respective dynamics of given cases, political shortsightedness, and interest politics. We require qualification and refinement of the arguments. Nonetheless the criticisms leveled here are fundamental and far-reaching.

The policy implications of these comments are also major. They mean the reexamination and likely restructuring of most of our aid and foreign assistance programs directed toward developing nations. They imply the shortsightedness and impropriety of seeking to apply European and North American strategies and institutional paraphernalia to societies and cultures where they simply do not fit. They imply that U.S. and international agency decision makers be much more circumspect in their assertion that they know best for the developing nations. Even more fundamental, these comments imply a considerable reeducation, in nonethnocentric understandings, of at least two generations of social scientists, policy makers, and the informed public, indeed of our educational focus, national ethos, and career system. One should probably not be optimistic.

Notes

1. The themes treated here complement those developed in Reinhard Bendix, "Tradition and Modernity Reconsidered," *Comparative Studies in Society and History,* 9 (April 1967), 292–346; reprinted in Bendix, *Embattled Reason* (New York: Oxford University Press, 1970). The present essay goes considerably beyond Bendix's argument, however, develops some distinctive propositions, and elaborates more far-reaching conclusions.

2. William P. Glade, "Problems of Research in Latin American Studies," in *New Directions in Language and Area Studies: Priorities for the 1980s* (Milwaukee: Center for Latin America, University of Wisconsin at Milwaukee for the Consortium of Latin American Studies Programs, CLASP, May 1979), pp. 81–101.

3. G. W. E. Hegel, *The Philosophy of History* (New York: Dover, 1956), p. 87; Shlomo Avineri, ed., *Karl Marx on Colonialism and Modernization* (Garden City, New York: Anchor, 1969); W. W. Rostow, *The Stages of Economic Growth: A Non-Communist Manifesto* (Cambridge: Cambridge University Press, 1960).

4. Robert A. Nisbet, *Social Change and History: Aspects of the Western Theory of Development* (Oxford: Oxford University Press, 1969).

5. See virtually any text, such as those by Hacker, Sabine, Wolin, etc.

6. Bernice Hamilton, *Political Thought in Sixteenth Century Spain* (Oxford: Oxford University Press, 1963); Guenter Lewy, *Constitutionalism and Statecraft during the Golden Age of Spain* (Geneva: Droz, 1960); Howard J. Wiarda, "Corporatist Theory and Ideology: A Latin American Development Paradigm," *Journal of Church and State,* vol. 20 (1970), pp. 29–56.

7. For more details see Bendix, "Tradition and Modernity"; and Howard J. Wiarda, "Corporatism and Development in the Iberic-Latin World: Persistent Strains and New Variations," *Review of Politics,* vol. 36 (January 1974), pp. 3–33.

8. See especially the writings of S. N. Eisenstadt, *e.g.,* "Post-Traditional Societies and the Continuity and Reconstruction of Tradition," *Daedalus,* vol. 102 (1973), pp. 1–27; and "Tradition, Change and Modernity: Modern Society and Sociological Theory" (unpublished).

9. For a volume that does encompass the smaller nations and advances an alternative, "corporative" European polity model, see Martin O. Heisler, ed., *Politics in Europe* (New York: McKay, 1974).

10. Frederick B. Pike and Thomas Stritch, eds., *The New Corporatism: Social-Political Structures in the Iberian World* (Notre Dame, Indiana: Notre Dame University Press, 1974); Howard J. Wiarda, *Corporatism and Development: The Portuguese Experience* (Amherst: University of Massachusetts Press, 1977).

11. See Howard J. Wiarda, "Toward a Framework for the Study of Political Change in the Iberic-Latin Tradition," *World Politics,* vol. 25 (January 1973), pp. 206–35; *From Corporatism to Neo-Syndicalism: The State, Organized Labor, and the Changing Industrial Relations Systems of Southern Europe* (Cambridge: Harvard University, Center for European Studies, 1981); and "Does Europe Still Stop at the Pyrenees or Does Latin America Begin There? Iberia, Latin America, and the Second Enlargement of the European Community" (Washington, D.C.: American Enterprise Institute, Center for Hemispheric Studies, Occasional Paper No. 2, 1982).

12. To start, see Paul E. Sigmund, ed., *The Ideologies of the Developing Nations* (New York: Praeger, 1972); W. A. Beling and G. O. Totten, eds., *Developing Nations: Quest for a Model* (New York: Van Nostrand, 1970); Howard J. Wiarda, *Politics and Social Change in Latin America: The Distinct Tradition* (Amherst: University of Massachusetts Press, 1982). See also the citations in the following chapter.

13. Examples include Daniel Lerner, *The Passing of Traditional Society* (New York: The Free Press, 1964); Wilbert E. Moore, *The Impact of Industry* (Engle-

wood Cliffs, N.J.: Prentice Hall, 1965); Clark Kerr *et al.*, *Industrialism and Industrial Man* (Cambridge: Harvard University Press, 1960); and Alex Inkeles and David H. Smith, *Becoming Modern* (Cambridge: Harvard University Press, 1974).

14. Raymond Aron, *Main Currents in Sociological Thought: Durkheim, Pareto, Weber* (Garden City, N. Y.: Anchor, 1970).

15. The analysis here and in the next three paragraphs derives in large measure from Thomas O. Wilkinson, "Family Structure and Industrialization in Japan," *American Sociological Review,* vol. 28 (October 1962), pp. 678–82; and his *The Urbanization of Japanese Labor* (Amherst: University of Massachusetts Press, 1965).

16. Talcott Parsons, *The Social System* (New York: The Free Press, 1951); *The Structure of Social Action* (New York: The Free Press, 1937); (with Edward Shils) *Toward a General Theory of Action* (Cambridge: Harvard University Press, 1951).

17. Gabriel A. Almond and James S. Coleman, eds., *The Politics of the Developing Areas* (Princeton: Princeton University Press, 1960). The other authors cited are so familiar as to require no specific references to their work.

18. The image is that of Philippe C. Schmitter, "Paths to Political Development in Latin America," in *Changing Latin America* (New York: Columbia University, Academy of Political Science, 1972), pp. 83–105.

19. Avineri, *Karl Marx,* Introduction; Bendix, "Tradition and Modernity."

20. The parallels in the rise and decline of such U.S.-sponsored programs as agrarian reform, community development, and family planning would make an interesting study.

21. These considerations of "historical space-time," a concept that has often confused U.S. observers, lay behind the efforts of Haya de la Torre and the Peruvian *Apristas* to develop an indigenous ideology for Latin America.

22. David Apter, *The Politics of Modernization* (Chicago: University of Chicago Press, 1965).

23. Anthony James Joes, *Fascism in the Contemporary World* (Boulder, Colo.: Westview Press, 1978); James Malloy, ed., *Authoritarianism and Corporatism in Latin America* (Pittsburgh: University of Pittsburgh Press, 1977).

24. Claudio Veliz, *The Centralist Tradition of Latin America* (Princeton: Princeton University Press, 1979); A. James Gregor, *Italian Fascism and Developmental Dictatorship* (Princeton: Princeton University Press, 1979); David Collier, ed., *The New Authoritarianism in Latin America* (Princeton: Princeton University Press, 1979).

25. Lloyd I. Rudolph and Susanne Hoeber Rudolph, *The Modernity of Tradition: Political Development in India* (Chicago: University of Chicago Press, 1967); Randall Stokes and Anthony Harris, "South African Development and the Paradox of Racial Particularism: Toward a Theory of Modernization from the Center," *Economic Development and Cultural Change,* vol. 26 (January 1978), pp. 245–69.

26. Howard J. Wiarda, *Critical Elections and Critical Coups: State, Society and the Military in the Processes of Latin American Development* (Athens: Center for International Studies, Ohio University, 1979).

27. The issue is discussed further in Howard J. Wiarda, "Democracy and

Human Rights in Latin America: Toward a New Conceptualization," *Orbis*, vol. 22 (1978), pp. 137–60.

28. My colleague Guenter Lewy is writing a book on "false consciousness"; I have profited from discussing the matter with him.

29. These themes are dealt with in greater detail in Howard J. Wiarda, ed., *The Continuing Struggle for Democracy in Latin America* (Boulder, Colo.: Westview Press, 1979).

30. For one such example, see Howard J. Wiarda, *Dictatorship, Development, and Disintegration: Politics and Social Change in the Dominican Republic* (Ann Arbor: Xerox University Microfilms Monograph Series, 1975).

31. Dillon Soares, "Latin American Studies in the United States: A Critique and a Proposal," *Latin American Research Review*, vol. II (1976), pp. 51–69.

32. In Lucian Pye and Sidney Verba, eds., *Political Culture and Political Development* (Princeton: Princeton University Press, 1965).

33. For such a *verstahen* approach and its effect *both* on the region studied and the researchers, see Jean Duvignaud, *Change at Shebika: Report from a North African Village* (New York: Pantheon, 1970).

34. Peter Winch, *The Idea of a Social Science and Its Relations to Philosophy* (London, 1960).

35. See chapter 3.

36. Samuel P. Huntington, in a personal conversation with the author; see also the volume edited by the author, *New Directions in Comparative Politics* (Boulder, Colo.: Westview Press, forthcoming), which grows out of a faculty seminar with the same title organized at the Center for International Affairs, Harvard University.

37. Howard J. Wiarda, "Toward a Framework"; *Politics and Social Change;* "The Latin Americanization of the United States," *The New Scholar*, vol. 7 (1977), pp. 51–85; and *Corporatism and National Development in Latin America* (Boulder, Colo.: Westview Press, 1981).

3

Toward a Nonethnocentric Theory of Development: Alternative Conceptions from the Third World

[The Ayatullah] Khomeini has blown apart the comfortable myth that as the Third World industrializes, it will also adopt Western values.

Time (January 7, 1980)

A revolution of far-reaching breadth and meaning is now sweeping the Third World, and we in the West are only partially and incompletely aware of it. This revolution carries immense implications not only for the Third World and our relations with it but also, more generally, for the social sciences and the way we comprehend and come to grips with Third World change.

We are all aware of the new social and economic forces of modernization sweeping the Third World and perhaps, to a somewhat lesser extent, of the political and value changes also occurring, including anti-Americanism and anticolonialism. What has received less attention is the way these changes are now finding parallel expression in a rejection of the basic developmental models and paradigms originating in the West, both Marxian and non-Marxian varieties, and a

A Senior Fellowship from the National Endowment for the Humanities provided research and writing assistance; the paper was written while the author was a Research Scholar at the Center for International Affairs, Harvard University. An earlier version of this chapter appeared in *The Journal of Developing Areas*, vol. 17, no. 4 (July 1983), pp. 433–52.

41

corresponding assertion of non-Western, nonethnocentric, and indigenous ones.[1]

The ongoing Iranian revolution may not be typical, but it is illustrative. At the popular level, awareness of the profound changes occurring in Iran was warped and obscured by events surrounding the revolution and the 1979 seizure of the American hostages, by the discomfort those in the more pluralist societies of the West feel toward the Islamic fundamentalists' assertion that there is a single right way and a wrong way to do everything, and by the general "ugliness" (at least as portrayed on our TV screens) of some of the revolution's leaders. Even scholars and others more sympathetic to such fundamental transformations, in Iran and elsewhere, have tended to focus on the changes occurring in their one area or country of specialization and have not analyzed the more general phenomenon or placed it in a broader, global perspective.[2] Alternatively, they have preferred to see the Iranian revolution and the coming to power of its ayatullah as an isolated event, readily subject to ridicule and agreed-upon moral outrage and therefore not representing a serious challenge to established Western values and social science understandings.

The proposition argued here, however, is that the rejection of the Western (that is, Northwest European and U.S.) model of development, in its several varieties, is now widespread throughout the Third World and that there are many new and exciting efforts on the part of intellectuals and political elites throughout these areas to assert new and indigenous models of development. Furthermore, these efforts represent serious and fundamental challenges to many cherished social science assumptions and understandings and even to the presumption of a universal social science of development. Thus, we underestimate or continue to disregard such changes at the risk of both perpetuating our poor comprehension of the Third World areas and retaining a social science of development that is parochial and ethnocentric rather than accurate and comprehensive.[3]

The Iranian revolution, with its assertion of Islamic fundamentalism and of a distinctively Islamic social science (or model) of development, is in fact but one illustration of a far more general Third World phenomenon. There are common themes in the reexaminations now under way by many Third World leaders: of Indian caste associations and their potential role in modernization; of African tribalism not as a traditional institution that is necessarily dysfunctional and therefore to be discarded but as a base upon which to build new kinds of societies; of Latin American organicism, corporatism, populism, and new forms of bureaucratic-authoritarianism or of democracy; of family and interpersonal solidarities in Japan; of the overlaps of Confucian

42

and Maoist conceptions in China. These themes relate to the hostility toward and often the inappropriateness of the Western developmental models in non-Western or only partially Western areas, the nationalistic and often quite original assertion of local and indigenous ones, and the questioning of some basic notions regarding the universality of the social sciences. They relate also to the realization that there are not just one or two (First and Second World) paths to development but many and diverse ones, and that the dichotomies between traditional and modern represent not real but false choices for societies where the blending and fusion of these is both likely and more widespread than the necessary or automatic replacement of the former by the latter.[4]

These themes are controversial and provocative, and not all the dimensions and issues can be dealt with here. Rather, my purposes are to present the critique Third World areas are now directing at the Western and, we often presume, universal developmental model; to examine the alternatives they themselves are now in the process of formulating; to assess the problems and difficulties in these alternative formulations; and to offer some conclusions regarding the issue of particularism versus universalism in the social sciences.

The Third World Critique of the Western Developmental Model

In all frankness, much of our self-inflicted disaster has its intellectual roots in our social sciences faculties.
West Indian economist Courtney N. Blackman,
in "Science, Development, and Being Ourselves,"
Caribbean Studies Newsletter (Winter 1980)

The Third World critique of the Western model and pattern of development as inappropriate and irrelevant, or partially so, to its circumstances and conditions is widespread and growing. There has long been a powerful strain of anti-Westernism (as well as anticolonialism) on the part of Third World intellectuals , but now that sentiment is stronger and well-nigh universal. The recent trends differ from the earlier critiques of Western modernization theory in that the attacks have become far more pervasive, they are shared more generally by the society as a whole, they have taken on global rather than simply area or country-specific connotations, and the criticisms are no longer solely negative but are now accompanied by an assertion of other, alternative, often indigenous approaches. Moreover, the debate is no longer just a scholarly one between competing social science development models; rather, it has powerful policy implications as well.

One should not overstate the case. As yet, the critiques one reads are frequently as inchoate and uncertain as the concept of the Third World itself. They tend sometimes to be partial and incomplete, fragmented and unsystematic, long on rhetoric but short on reality, often as nationalistic and parochial as the very Western theories they seek to replace. Yet one cannot but be impressed by the growing strength of these critiques, the increasing acceptance and receptivity of them by Third World leaders, and the dawning realization of common themes, criticisms, and problems encountered with the Western model across diverse continents, nations, and cultural traditions. Let us reiterate briefly the arguments of the previous chapter.

The criticism centers, to begin with, on the bias and ethnocentrism perceived in the Western model and on its inapplicability to societies with quite different traditions, histories, societies, and cultural patterns.[5] For societies cast in traditions other than the Judeo-Christian, lacking the sociopolitical precepts of Greece, Rome, and the Bible, without the same experiences of feudalism and capitalism, the argument is that the Western model has only limited relevance.[6] Western political theory, we have seen, is faulted for its almost entirely European focus and its complete lack of attention to other intellectual traditions. Political sociology in Durkheim, Comte, Weber, or Parsons is shown to be based almost exclusively on the European transition from agrarian society to industrial society and its accompanying sociopolitical effects, which have proved somewhat less than universal.[7] Finally, political economy, in both its Marxian and non-Marxian variants, is criticized for the exclusively European and hence less-than-universal origins of its major precepts: philosophical constructs derived (especially in Marx) from Germany, a conception of sociopolitical change derived chiefly from the French tradition, and an understanding of industrialization and its effects stemming chiefly from the English experience. Even our celebrated liberal arts education (basically Western European) has come in for criticism because it is not an experience of universal relevance but merely the first area studies program.[8] These criticisms of the narrowness and parochialism of our major social science traditions and concepts, as grounded essentially on the singular experience of Western Europe and without appreciation of or applicability to the rest of the world, are both sweeping and, with proper qualification, persuasive.

Third World intellectuals have begun to argue, second, that the timing, sequence, and stages of development in the West may not necessarily be replicable in their own areas. Again, this argument is not new, but its sophisticated expression by so many Third World leaders is. For example, Western political sociology generally asserts, based on the European experience, that bureaucratization and urban-

44

ization accompanied and were products of industrialization; in Latin America and elsewhere, however, many Third World scholars are arguing that the phenomena of preindustrial urbanization and bureaucratization would seem to require different kinds of analyses.[9] With regard to timing, it seems obvious that countries developing and modernizing in the late twentieth century should face different kinds of problems from those that developed in the nineteenth; because their developmental response must necessarily be different, there seems to be no reason why the former should merely palely and retardedly repeat the experience of the latter.[10] In terms of stages, the European experience would lead us to believe that capitalism must necessarily replace feudalism. In much of the Third World, however, feudalism in accord with the classic French case seems never to have existed;[11] capitalism exists in forms (populist, patrimonialist, and etatist) that hardly existed in the West; and rather than capitalism definitely *replacing* feudalism, it seems more likely that the two will continue to exist side by side. The timing, sequences, and stages of development in most Third World nations are sufficiently different, indeed, that virtually all our Western precepts require fundamental reinterpretation when applied there: the so-called demographic transition, the role of the emerging middle classes, military behavior and professionalization, the role of peasants and workers, the presumption of greater pluralism as societies develop, notions of differentiation and rationalization, and so on.[12]

Not only are the timing, sequences, and stages of Third World development likely to be quite different, but the international context is entirely altered as well. In the nineteenth century, countries like Britain, Japan, and the United States were able to develop relatively autonomously; for today's Third World nations, that is no longer possible. To cite only a handful of many possible illustrations, these nations are often caught up in Cold War struggles over which they have no control and in which they are cast as mere pawns; they are absolutely dependent on outside capital, technology, and markets for their products;[13] and they are part of an international community and of a web of international military, diplomatic, political, commercial, cultural, communications, and other ties from which they cannot divorce themselves. Moreover, many of them, entirely dependent for their continued development on external energy sources, are thus the victims of skyrocketing prices that they can ill afford to pay and that have wreaked havoc with their national economies. In these and other ways it seems clear that the international context of development is entirely different from that of a century to a century and a half ago.

A fourth area of difference perceived by leaders from the Third

World relates to the role of traditional institutions. Western political sociology largely assumes that such traditional institutions as tribes, castes, clans, patrimonialist authority, and historical corporate units must either yield and give way (the liberal tradition) under the impact of modernization or be overwhelmed (the revolutionary tradition) by it. Nevertheless, we have learned that in much of the Third World so-called traditional institutions have, first of all, proved remarkably resilient, persistent, and long-lasting; rather than fading or being crushed under the impact of change, they have proved flexible, accommodative, and adaptive, bending to the currents of modernization but not being replaced by them.[14] Second, these traditional institutions have often served as filters of the modernization process, accepting what was useful and what they themselves could absorb in modernity while rejecting the rest. Third, we have learned that such traditional institutions as India's caste associations, African tribalism, and Latin American corporatism can often be transformed into agents of modernization, bridging some wrenching transitions and even serving as the base for new and more revered forms of indigenous development.[15] Indeed one of the more interesting illustrations of this process is the way a new generation of African leaders, rather than rejecting tribalism as traditional and to be discarded, as the *geist* of Western political sociology would have them do, are now reexamining tribalism's persistent presence as an indigenous, realistic, and perhaps viable base on which to construct a new kind of authentic African society.[16]

Fifth, Third World intellectuals are beginning to argue that the Eurocentrism of the major development models has skewed, biased, and distorted their own and the outside world's understanding of Third World societies and has made them into something of a laughingstock, the butt of cruel, ethnic, and sometimes racial gibes. For example, the Western bias had led scholars, those from the West and sometimes those from the Third World, to study and over emphasize such presumably modernizing institutions as professional associations and political parties; yet in many Third World countries these institutions may not count for very much, and their absence or weakness, or the quite distinct roles they may play, often leads these societies to be labeled underdeveloped or dysfunctional. At the same time, as we saw in the previous chapter, institutions that Western political sociology has proclaimed traditional and hence inevitably fated to die or disappear, such as patronage networks, clan groups, religious institutions and movements, extended families and the like, have been woefully understudied and represent some immense gaps in our knowledge concerning these societies. Consequently, there exist some fundamental misinterpretations of them.[17]

Meanwhile, these nations actually do modernize and develop, in their terms if not always in ours—that is, through coups and barracks revolts that sometimes contribute to an expanding circulation of elites, through larger patronage and spoils systems now transferred to the national level, through assistance from abroad that is often employed not entirely inappropriately in ways other than those intended, and through elaborated corporate group, family, clan and/or tribal networks. Yet the actual dynamics of change and modernization in these nations have often been made the stuff of *opéra bouffe* in *New York Times* headlines or *New Yorker* cartoons or have led to appalled or holier-than-thou attitudes on the part of Westerners who would still like to remake the Third World in accord with Judeo-Christian morality and Anglo-American legal and political precepts. The excessive attention to some institutions that our often wishful sociology would elevate to a higher plane than they deserve, the neglect of others, and our ethnocentrism and general ignorance as to how Third World societies do in fact develop have perpetuated our woeful misunderstanding and inadequate comprehension of them.[18] Indeed, it is one of the greater ironies that for a long time Third World intellectuals bought, or were sold, the same essentially Western categories as the Westernizers themselves had internalized and that their understanding of their own societies therefore was often no greater than our own. That condition is now changing very rapidly.[19]

The Western development perspective, furthermore, has recently been subjected to an additional criticism: that it is part of the Western ideological and intellectual offensive to keep the Third World within the Western orbit.[20] This is perhaps the most widespread of the criticisms of the Western development model current in the Third World. Western modernization and development theory is thus seen as still another "imperialist" Cold War strategy aimed at tying Third World nations into a Western and liberal (that is, U.S.) development pattern, of keeping them within our sphere of influence, and of denying them the possibilities of alternative developmental patterns. Of course, it should be said that not all of those who fashioned the early and influential development literature had such manifest Cold War or New Mandarin goals in mind. Some clearly did,[21] but among others the development literature was popular chiefly because it corresponded to cherished notions about ourselves (that we are a liberal, democratic, pluralist, socially just, and modern nation) and to the belief that the developing nations could emulate us if they worked hard and recast themselves in accord with the American or Western way. This strategy, one would have to say, was remarkably successful from the

47

late 1950s, when the first development literature began to appear, until the early 1970s. Since that time, however, the development literature has been increasingly tarred with the imperialist brush and discredited throughout the Third World, and hence a whole new generation of young Third World leaders and intellectuals no longer accepts the Western developmentalist concepts and perspectives and is searching for possible alternatives.[22]

Finally, and perhaps most harmful in terms of the long-term development of the Third World, is the damage that has been inflicted on their own institutions because of the Western biases. "Development" is no mere intellectual construct, nor is it benignly neutral. There are consequences, often negative, in following a Western-oriented development strategy. Here we have in mind not just the damage inflicted on such countries as the Dominican Republic by Cold War rivalries and U.S. intervention (1965), or by such agencies as the International Monetary Fund, whose financial advice to Third World nations has often been unenlightened. Instead what concerns us here is the role development has had in undermining such viable traditional institutions as extended family networks, patronage ties, clan and tribal loyalties, corporate group links, churches and religious movements, historical authority relations, and the like. By eroding and often eliminating these traditional institutions before any more modern ones were created, development helped destroy some of the only agencies in many Third World nations that might have enabled them to make a genuine transition to real modernity. The destruction, in the name of modernization, of these kinds of traditional institutions throughout the Third World may well be one of the most important legacies that development left behind, and it will powerfully affect our future relations with them. For by our actions and our patronizing, condescending, and ethnocentric efforts to promote development among the LDCs, we may have inadvertently denied them the possibility of real development while at the same time erasing the very indigenous and at one time viable institutions they are now attempting, perhaps futilely and too late, to resurrect.[23]

The Third World critique of the Western development model as biased, ethnocentric, and often damaging is thus strong, sweeping, and, in its essentials, difficult to refute. Although many of the arguments are not new and though not all Third World critiques are as coherent, global, and organized as presented here, the criticisms are spreading and becoming universal, the common elements are being analyzed, and they are increasingly informed by solid facts and argument. It remains for us to examine what the Third World offers in place of the Western schema.

The Assertion of Indigenous Third World Development Models

The problem with us Africans is that we've not been educated to appreciate our art and culture. So many of us have been influenced by the British system of education. I went through this system here not knowing enough about my own country. It was almost as if what we natives did wasn't important enough to be studied. I knew all about British history and British art, but about Ghana and Africa nothing.

Ghanaian art historian and intellectual Nana Apt, quoted in *New York Times*, September 13, 1980, p. 16

The purpose of this section is to provide a sense of the kinds and varieties of new development models emerging from the Third World. Space constraints rule out any detailed treatment here; our survey provides only a hint of the new ideas, concepts, and theories.[24] Nevertheless, even in a brief passage it is possible to convey some of the main themes from each of the major areas, to show their common currents, and to begin to analyze the larger patterns. More detailed treatment is reserved for a planned book-length study.[25]

In his influential work *Beyond Marxism: Towards an Alternative Perspective*, Indian political theorist Vrajenda Raj Mehta argues that neither liberal democracy nor communism is an appropriate framework for Indian development. He attributes their inadequacy to their unidimensional views of man and society. The liberal-democratic view that man is a consumer of utilities and producer of goods serves to legitimize a selfish, atomistic, egoistic society. Communism, he says, reduces all human dimensions to one, the economic, and transforms all human activity into one, state activity, which erodes all choice and destroys life's diversities.[26]

Mehta further argues for a multidimensional conception of man and society incorporating (1) the objective, external, rational; (2) the subjective, internal, intuitive; (3) the ethical, normative, harmonious; and (4) the spiritual and fiduciary. For the development of man's multidimensional personality, society must be structured as an "oceanic circle," an integral-pluralist system of wholes within wholes. The four social wholes of Mehta's well-organized society consist of "those devoted to the pursuit of knowledge, those who run the administration and protect the community from external aggression, those who manage the exchange of services of goods, and those who attend to manual and elementary tasks" (p. 54). Mehta claims that such an integralist-pluralist order will overcome the atomistic limitations of liberal democracy and the economic and bureaucratic collectivism of communism. The logic of "developing wholes" means that each sector of society must have autonomy or *swaraj* within an overall system of harmony and oceanic circles. Emphasizing both the autonomy of the several societal sectors and their integration within a larger whole, Mehta calls this essentially Indian-organic-corporatist system "integral pluralism":

> Integral pluralism insists that the development of society has to be the development of the whole society. The whole is not one, but itself consists of various wholes, of economics and politics, ethics, and religion, as also of different types of individuals. The relationship of each of them to each other is in the nature of oceanic circles (p. 60).

Particularly interesting for our purposes are Mehta's attempts to ground his theory in the reality of Indian culture, history, and civilization. "Each national community," he says, "has its own law of development, its own way to fulfill itself." "The broken mosaic of Indian society," he goes on, "cannot be recreated in the image of the West—India must find its own strategy of development and nation-building suited to its own peculiar conditions" (p. 92). Instead of being dazzled by the national progress of the West and futilely trying to emulate its development model, India should define its goals and choose its means "separately in terms of its own resources and the role it wants to play on the world scene." Rejecting the thesis of a single and universal pattern of development, Mehta advocates an indigenous process of change attuned to the needs of individual societies: "A welcome process of social change in all societies is a process towards increasing self-awareness in terms of certain normatively defined goals in each case, and that the direction of the process and the definition of ends is largely defined by the society's own distinct history and way of life" (p. 104).

Mehta's theory of integral pluralism is a bold and erudite exposition of a model of indigenous development for India. Although he draws some of his ideas eclectically from the West, the specific sources of inspiration for his model are Indian: the Vedic seers, the *Mahabharata*, Tagore, and Gandhi. In contemporary India the model derives particular support from nationalists and from those who advocate the Gandhian model of development, which emphasizes a decentralized economy based on small industries, a reorientation of production in terms of criteria besides prosperity only, a possible decentralized defense industry, and hence a particularly Indian route to development.

Mehta believes that the form of liberal democracy derived from England, the colonial power, is inappropriate and unworkable in the

Indian context. Political events in India in recent years would seem to provide abundant through still incomplete evidence for that argument. But neither is communism in accord with India's traditions, he argues. Mehta states that the crisis in Indian politics is due to the fact that the constitution and political system are not based on what he calls the "hidden springs" or the underlying institutional and cultural heritage of Indian society. That is why, he writes, there are presently disillusionment, institutional atrophy, spreading chaos, and a concomitant widespread desire to adopt the Gandhian model. Accordingly, the successful ruler and developer in the Indian context

> will be the one who will not only have an idea of the system of international stratification and the position of the dominant powers in it, but also the one who will weave into a holistic view the fact that his society once had a glorious civilization which, due to certain structural defects and rigidities, gave way to conquerors from the outside; he will be conscious of the continuity amidst all the shifts in the historical scene, of the underlying unity amongst a panorama of immense and baffling diversities (p. 115).

No claim is made here that Mehta's book captures the essence of contemporary Indian thinking or that it is necessarily representative of the newer currents emanating from Indian intellectuals or public opinion.[27] It is, nevertheless, illustrative of the kind of thinking and writing now beginning to emerge, and there is no doubt that its clarion call for a nationalistic and indigenous model of development has struck in his country an immensely responsive chord. Moreover, it corresponds closely to other observed phenomena in contemporary India: the increased repudiation of English and Western influences, the rising tide of Indian nationalism, the revival of various religious movements and the corresponding criticisms of Western secularism and pluralism, the justifications for authoritarian rule and of integral and harmonious development, and the reinterpretation of caste associations no longer as traditional institutions that must be destroyed but as indigenous agencies capable themselves of modernization and of serving as transitional bridges of development. These deep-rooted trends help make Mehta's book and the voluminous writings of numerous other scholars and popularizers worthy of serious attention.[28]

The new and often parallel currents stirring the Islamic world have received far more popular attention than have those in India. There can be no doubt that a major religious revival is sweeping the world of Islam,[29] but our understanding of the forces at work has been obscured, biased, and retarded by events in Iran and by general Western hostility to them. It is relatively easy in the Iranian case to express our appalled indignation at the summary trials and executions, the brutal treatment of the American hostages, and the sometimes wild fulminations of an aging ayatullah. By doing so, however, we may miss some of the deeper, permanent, and more important aspects of the changes under way.[30]

Two major features of the Islamic revival command special attention here. Both are also present in the Indian case . One is the criticism of the Western models, either liberal or communist, as inappropriate and undesirable in the Islamic context. The widespread sentiment in favor of rejecting Western values and the Western developmental model has again been obscured in the popular media by their focusing only on the sometimes ludicrous comments of Iran's religious leaders that the Western model is sinful and satanic. That focus makes it easy to satirize, parody, and dismiss what is, in fact, a widespread criticism and which, coming from other Islamic sources—in, for instance, Saudi Arabia and Pakistan—is quite realistic and telling. The argument is that the excessive individualism of the liberal model and the excessive statism of the communist one are both inappropriate in the Islamic context: they violate its customs and traditions by importing a system without strong indigenous roots, and they are positively damaging in terms of the Islamic world's own preferred values and institutions.[31]

The second aspect commanding attention, complementary to the first, is the effort on the part of the Iranians and others, once the Western influences were excised or repudiated, to reconstruct society and polity on the bases of indigenous and Islamic concepts and institutions. Once more, what is in fact a serious process has frequently been made ludicrous in the media where only the comic-opera and the most brutal aspects have received attention. But surely the efforts to reforge the links between the state and society that had been largely destroyed by the Shah, to lay stress on the family, the local community, a corporate group life and solidarity, and the leader who provides both direction and moral values—in contrast to the alienation and mass society that are among the more visible results of the Western pattern of development—are serious and therefore must command our attention. Important too are the efforts at religious revival and the attempts to reconstruct law, society, and behavior in accord with religious and moral principles, to rejoin politics and ethics in ways that in the West have been nearly irrevocably broken since Machiavelli. Rather than reject such developments out of hand, which further postpones our understanding of them, Westerners must begin to take Islamic society on its own terms, not from the point of view of automatic rejection or a haughty sense of superiority, but with empathy and understanding. Indeed one of the more fascinating aspects that has emerged from this Islamic revival is not only a set of new, innovative, and indigenous institutions but a whole, distinctive Islamic social science of development to go with it.[32]

In Africa the institution around which the discussion revolves is tribalism. Tribalism is one of those traditional institutions, like India's caste associations or Islamic fundamentalism, that was supposed to decline or disappear as modernization went forward . This sentiment was so deeply ingrained that African leaders themselves were often made to feel ashamed of their own backgrounds and origins. Tribalism had to be repressed and denied and the nation-state or the single party mass-mobilizing system elevated to an artificial importance, which in fact it did not have.[33] When tribalism refused to die, it was rebaptized under the rubric of ethnicity and ethnic conflict, which somehow made it seem more modern.

There are still Westerners and Africans alike who would deny the existence of tribalism and would seek to stamp it out, but among other Africans there is a new and refreshing realism about tribalism, even some interesting albeit not as yet overly successful efforts to reconstruct African society using tribalism as a base. These attempts include new variations on the federal principle, new forms of consociationalism, a corporately based communalism as in Tanzania, or the African authenticity of Zaire. Whatever the precise name and form, these newer approaches to tribalism would seem to be both more realistic and more interesting than the past denial of or wishful thinking about it.

At a minimum, the tribe often gives people what little they have in rural Africa: a patch of land for their huts and maize, leadership, order, and coherence. The tribe often has its own police force, which offers a measure of security. In countries sometimes without effective national welfare or social security, tribal authority and tradition help provide for the old and sick. Tribal ties and solidarities in the cities also help provide jobs, patronage, and positions within the army or bureaucracy. Parties and interest associations are often organized along tribal lines. In the absence of strong states and national political structures, the tribe may be an effective intermediary association providing services and brokering relations between the individual, family, or clan and the national government. Hence while tribalism may weaken over time, it surely will not disappear, and there is a growing and realistic recognition on the part of African leaders that tribalism is part of Africa. Many will find this new realism refreshing and the effort to refashion African polities and social structures in accord with its own indigenous traditions exciting and innovative.[34]

The case of Latin America is somewhat different since it is an area that we think of as already Western.[35] Properly qualified (taking into account Latin America's large indigenous populations, the periodic efforts to resurrect and glorify its Indian past, or the efforts of nations such as Mexico to ground their nationalism in part upon their mestizoness—the new "cosmic race"), this assertion is valid. One must also remember, however, that Latin America is an offshoot or historical fragment of a special time and of a special part of the West, Iberia circa 1500,[36] whose own conformity to the Western model has been and in many ways still is somewhat less than 100 percent.[37] With this in mind, we may look on Latin America as something of a mixed case, Western and Third World at the same time.

In various writings I have wrestled with this issue of where and in what ways Latin America conforms to the Western pattern and where it is distinctive.[38] In the context of this discussion, however, what is striking are the remarkable parallels between the newer currents in Latin America and those in other Third World areas. First, there is a growing nationalistic rejection of the U.S.-favored route to development, a rejection that has even stronger historical roots than in other Third World areas and that found expression as early as the nineteenth century in fears and hostility toward the "colossus of the north" and in the widespread acceptance of the arguments of José E. Rodó, who contrasted the spiritualism, Catholicism, personalism, and humanism of Latin America (Ariel) with the crassness, materialism, secularism, pragmatism, and utilitarianism of the United States (Caliban).[39]

Second, and the reverse side of this coin, is the effort to identify what is distinctive in Latin America's own past and present and to determine whether these characteristics can be used to erect a separate Latin American political sociology of development. Such a formulation would emphasize Latin America's persistent corporatism and organic statism, its neomercantilist and state-capitalist economic structures, its personalism and kinship patterns, its Catholicism and the institutions and behavioral patterns of Catholic political culture, its patrimonialism and unabashed patriarchalism, its patron-client networks now extended to the national political level, its distinctive patterns and arenas of state-society relations, and its historic relations of dependency (particularly in recent times) vis-à-vis the United States.[40] There are, as we shall see in the next section, problems with these formulations, not the least of which is that not all Latin Americans accept them or wish to accept them, still preferring to see themselves in terms of the Western model and still preferring to cast their lot with that model. Nevertheless, the parallels with other Third World areas are striking, and the attempts by Latin Americans to fashion their own indigenous model and social science of development must command our attention.

Analogous developments in other areas also merit serious study, though here only passing mention can be made of them. In China, for example, the combination of Marxist and Confucian elements in Mao's thought provided not only a new and fascinating synthesis but also some of the key ingredients in the distinctively Chinese model of development.[41] Japan has achieved phenomenal economic growth rates by borrowing, copying, or synthesizing the technology and organizational models of the West and adapting these to historical and preferred Japanese forms, structures, and ways of doing things.[42] In Poland and elsewhere in Eastern Europe, Marxism is being adapted to local and home-grown institutions such as Catholicism and nationalism. In the Soviet Union there is of course a Marxist socialist state, but no one would disagree it is also a *Russian* Marxist state (however ambiguous and open to disagreement may be its precise meaning).[43] Finally, in Western Europe itself, in whose development patterns the Western model obviously originated, there is both a new questioning of what the Western model consists of and whether even the nations of Western Europe conform to it, as well as a rethinking of whether that Western model is in fact applicable to the rest of the world.[44]

These various national and regional traditions need to be examined in detail and the arguments more fully amplified. What seems clear even from this brief survey, however, is that there is a growing rejection of the Western model as irrelevant and inappropriate in areas and nations where the traditions and institutions are quite different and that there exists a growing search for indigenous national institutions and models, based on local traditions instead of those imported from or imposed by the West. These trends seem now to cut across and transcend national and cultural boundaries.

Problem Areas and Dilemmas

The notion of a bright new world made up of young emerging nations is a fairy tale.
V.S. Naipaul, *Among the Believers*

There can be no doubt that the idea of a native, indigenous model and social science of development, reflecting and deeply rooted in local practices and institutions, is enormously attractive. Social scientists need to analyze this rather than merely celebrate it, however, and when that is done, numerous problems arise.

First, the search for indigenous models of development may prove to be more romantic and nostalgic than realistic.[45] In some areas and nations (several of the Central American countries, for example), indigenous institutions may well prove weak or nonexistent, incapable of serving as the base for national development. They may, as with the Western model, reflect the preferences of intellectuals rather than those of the general population—or they may reflect the nostalgic longing for a past that no longer exists and cannot be recreated. Such indigenous institutions may have been destroyed in whole or in part by the colonial powers or discredited by the earlier generation of Western-oriented local elites. There may not be an institutional foundation based on indigenous institutions and practices on which to build and hence, for many Third World nations, no light of whatever sort at the end of the development tunnel. The Western model seems not to have worked well, but an indigenous one may not work out either if it reflects the politics of romance and nostalgia rather than the politics of reality.[46]

Second, there are class, partisan, and other biases often implicit in a political strategy that seeks to fashion a model of development based upon indigenous institutions. Such a strategy may serve (though it need not necessarily do so) as a means to defend an existing status quo or to restore a status quo ante, both nationally and internationally. It may serve to justify an existing class, caste, leadership group, or clan remaining in power. It may be manipulated for partisan or personal advantage. For example, in Francisco Franco's efforts to restore and maintain traditional historic Spanish institutions and practices, it was clear that only his rather narrow and particular interpretation of what that special tradition was would be allowed and that other currents and possibilities within that tradition would be suppressed.[47]

Third, the actual practice of regimes that have followed an indigenous development strategy has not produced very many successes. Even on its own terms, it is hard to call the Iranian revolution, so far, a success. The Mexican revolution that was once trumpeted as providing an indigenous third way is acknowledged to have sold out, run its course, or died.[48] There has been a lot of talk about African authenticity in recent years, but in countries such as Togo or Zaire the application of the concept has served mainly to shore up corrupt and despotic regimes. Even in Tanzania, which has been widely cited as an example of a serious attempt to build an original African development model, there are immense difficulties accompanying this experiment and a notable lack of enthusiasm on the part of both the peasants who are presumably its prime beneficiaries and the government officials charged with implementing it.[49]

Fourth, it may be that in the present circumstances such indigenous developmental models are no longer possible. The time when a nation could maintain itself in isolation and could develop autonomously may well have passed. All of the Third World is now affected by global trends and movements.[50] These countries are also caught up in what Immanuel Wallerstein called the "world system"—factors such as trade patterns, economic dependency relationships, world market prices, oil requirements, and so on, which have major effects on them but over which they have no control.[51] In addition, whether one speaks of Afghanistan, El Salvador, or numerous other Third World nations, they are often involved in Cold War and other international political conflicts that cast them as pawns in the global arena and often affect in major ways their internal development as well. All these conditions make it virtually impossible for the outside world not to impinge on any effort at indigenous development, if not destroying it then certainly requiring compromise in numerous areas.[52]

Not only does the outside world impose itself, but, fifth, indigenous elites and intellectuals are not all convinced that they wish to follow such a native path. For them, traditional and indigenous institutions are not necessarily symbols of pride and nationalism but of backwardness and underdevelopment. Or they may have mixed feelings that breed confusion, irresolution, and lack of direction. Not all African leaders by any means are convinced that tribalism can serve as a new basis of political organization; hence in Kenya and elsewhere concerted efforts are under way not to build it up but to snuff it out. Indian intellectuals, especially from the lower castes, do not as yet seem ready to accept the arguments concerning the modernizing role the castes may play. Not all Iranian intellectuals accept the virtues of a theocratic state led by the Ayatullah or, even if they are believers in Islamic fundamentalism, are agreed on what precise institutional form that should take.

Latin America is an especially interesting area in this regard, for while most of its intellectuals share varying degrees of antipathy to the U.S. model and the U.S.-favored development route and want to have a hand in fashioning a nationalistic and Latin American one, they are also terribly uncomfortable with the implications of that position. That new route would imply acceptance of a political system built in some degree upon the principles of corporatism, hierarchy, authoritarianism, and organic-statism—none of which are popular or fashionable in the more democratic nations and salons of the modern world, into which Latin America and its intellectuals, historically plagued by a sense of inferiority and backwardness, also wish to be accepted. Hence they have ambivalent feelings regarding indigenous models and prefer theories of dependency or international stratification that conveniently and more comfortably place the blame on external instead of internal forces.[53]

Sixth and finally, emphasis must be placed on the sheer diversity of these nations and areas and hence the immense difficulties of achieving a consensus on any development strategy, whether indigenous or otherwise. At some levels of analysis, Latin America (and Iberia) may be thought of as part of a single cultural area, but it must also be kept in mind that Paraguay is quite different from Argentina, Brazil and Peru from Chile, Nicaragua from Mexico—and that all are at different levels of development. Hence different strategies and models of modernization, even if they could be conceptualized along certain common lines, would have to be designed for each country of the area.[54] In the Islamic world the same qualifications would have to be introduced; it obviously also makes a major difference if we are talking of the Sunni, the Shiite, or other traditions and combinations of them.[55] A similar case exists in Africa: some observers feel that Islam is the only organized cultural and ideological force capable of offering a coherent and continent-wide alternative to the heretofore dominant Western model. This point of view, however, ignores the still-strong Christian and Western influences, the fact that only a small minority of African states are essentially Muslim (that is, at least 75 percent Islamic), the continuing influence of traditional beliefs, and the fact that parts of Africa have no strong cultural identity of any sort. All of these and many other diversities and differentiations would have to be taken into account in creating for each of these areas an indigenous model, or models, of development. Nor should one underestimate the sheer confusion, uncertainty, and chaos surrounding these issues in many Third World nations. For the Third World as a whole and for its component geographic regions and distinct cultural areas, there is too much diversity to be subsumed under any one single theory or set of concepts.

Conclusion: Toward a Nonethnocentric Theory of Development

The aspiration for something different, better, more truly indigenous than Western systems of development and yet as socially and materially effective is palpable everywhere. "Our own way" is the persistent theme; but it is far more often advanced as a creed than as a plan.

Flora Lewis, *New York Times*, December 31, 1979

In numerous areas, the West and the Western model of development intimately associated with its earlier progress seem to be in decline. Western Europe suffers from various malaises of uncertain and often obscure origins, the economies of the Western nations have experienced severe recessions, American institutions have not always worked well in recent years, NATO and the Western Alliance are in disarray, and the global system of American hegemony and dominance is being challenged. With this Spenglerian "Decline of the West"[56] has also come a new questioning of and challenge to the development model that was a part of the nearly 500-year-long Western era of domination. It is not just the model itself that is now being challenged, however, but the larger, preeminently Western, and for that reason parochial and ethnocentric, philosophical and intellectual tradition that went with it. What we in the West, because our entire lifespans and those of our intellectual forebears were entirely encompassed within this time frame, assumed to be a universal set of norms and processes by which societies developed and modernized, and of which the West was presumably the leader and model, has now been demonstrated to be somewhat less than that.

With the decline of Western hegemony and the pretension to universalism of the intellectual constructs that are part and parcel of it, and concomitantly with the rise and new assertiveness of various non-Western and Third World areas, has also come the demand for local, indigenous models of development. The critique of the Western model as particularistic, parochial, Eurocentric, considerably less than universal, and hopelessly biased, as not only perpetuating our lack of understanding regarding these areas but also of wreaking downright harm upon them, seems devastating, persuasive, and perhaps unchallengeable. The question is no longer whether the Western model applies or whether it is salvageable but what is the precise nature of the models that have risen to take its place and whether these new models are functional and viable in terms of the Third World areas from which they are emerging.

These issues would seem to represent the next great frontier in the social sciences.[57] Shorn of its romantic and nostalgic aspects, unfettered by the class or partisan biases that sometimes surround it, incorporating both national currents and international ones, taking account of practical realities and not just intellectual constructs, cognizant of both the mixed sentiments of the local elites and the diversities of the societies studied—or at least recognizing these when they do occur—the notion of a nonethnocentric theory of development is now on the front burner. The study of such local, indigenous, native cultural traditions and models, Samuel P. Huntington has said, may well be the wave of the future for the social sciences.[58]

We need now for the first time to take non-Western areas and their often peculiar institutions seriously, in their own context and traditions rather than from the slanted perspective of the Western social sciences. We need, hence, to reexamine virtually all our Western social science notions of development. A serious mistake made by Western scholars, for example, is to assume that as people become modernized and educated, they also become Westernized. In fact in much of the Middle East, urbanization and the growth of a literate middle class are prime causes in the growth of interest in Islam. The examples could easily be multiplied. Hence, we need to see local indigenous institutions not necessarily as dysfunctional or anachronistic but frequently as viable and necessary in the society we are studying, as filters and winnowers of the modernization process, as agencies of transition between traditional and modern, and as means for reconciling and blending the global with the indigenous, the nationalist with the international. Such an undertaking implies both greater empathy on our part and greater modesty in terms of the claims made for the universalism of the Western examples.

The implications of such a recognition of indigenous institutions and of nonethnocentric theories and concepts of development are enormous.[59] Three major areas of impact may be noted here. The first has to do with the Third World and non-Western nations themselves: their efforts to overcome historical inferiority complexes, their reconceived possibilities for development, the new-found importance of their traditional institutions, the rediscovery of many and complex routes to development, their new sense of pride and accomplishment, and so on. It will take some time before the Third World is able to articulate and mold these diverse concepts into viable and realistic development models; the translation of concepts like authenticity into concrete political institutions, educational policies, health programs, and the like is likely to take even longer. Nevertheless, we cannot doubt the reality or growth of such new interpretations, outlooks, perspectives, and syntheses—as between Marxism and an indigenous development tradition, for example, or in the form of a homegrown type of democracy, or as an updated and modernized Islam.

Second, the arguments presented here have immense implications for the social sciences. Not only must we reexamine a host of essentially Western social science assumptions but we must also be prepared to accept a variety of regional, national, and cultural area-specific social sciences of development, and to strike some new balances between what is particular in the development process and what does in fact conform to more universal patterns. In exploring

60

such indigenous models, we will need to fashion a dynamic theory of change as well as to examine a variety of normative orientations;[60] we will need also to distinguish between a theory of development that comes from many sources and different theories of development for different regions. In the process the rather tired, even moribund, study of development itself, in all its dimensions, is likely to be revived.

Third, there are major implications for policy. In the past three decades not only have virtually all our intellectual concepts and models with regard to developing nations been based upon the Western experience, but virtually all our assistance programs, developmental recommendations, and foreign policy presumptions have been grounded on these same conceptual tools.[61] Hence the approach here suggested is likely to upset many cherished social science notions and, if considered seriously, will necessitate a fundamental set of foreign policy reconsiderations as well.

Notes

1. P. T. Bauer, *Dissent on Development* (Cambridge, Mass.: Harvard University Press, 1976); David E. Schmitt, ed., *Dynamics of the Third World* (Cambridge, Mass.: Winthrop, 1974); Frank Tachau, ed., *The Developing Nations: What Path to Modernization?* (New York: Dodd, Mead, 1972); W. A. Beling and G. O. Totten, eds., *The Developing Nations: Quest for a Model* (New York: Van Nostrand, 1970); Robert E. Gamer, *The Developing Nations* (Boston: Allyn and Bacon, 1976); Lyman Tower Sargent, *Contemporary Political Ideologies* (Homewood, Ill.: Dorsey, 1981); Paul E. Sigmund, ed., *The Ideologies of the Developing Nations* (New York: Praeger, 1972); John Kenneth Galbraith, *The Voice of the Poor* (Cambridge, Mass.: Harvard University Press, 1982); and Howard J. Wiarda, ed., *New Directions in Comparative Politics* (Boulder, Colo.: Westview Press, forthcoming).

2. For example, Edward Said, *Orientalism* (New York: Pantheon, 1978); Howard J. Wiarda, ed., *Politics and Social Change in Latin America: The Distinct Tradition*, 2nd ed. rev. (Amherst: University of Massachusetts Press, 1982).

3. These arguments are expanded in Howard J. Wiarda, "The Ethnocentrism of the Social Sciences: Implications for Research and Policy," *The Review of Politics*, vol. 42 (April 1981), pp. 163–97; chapter 2 in this study.

4. For some parallel arguments see Reinhard Bendix, "Tradition and Modernity Reconsidered," *Comparative Studies in Society and History*, vol. 9 (April 1967), pp. 292–346, reprinted in his *Embattled Reason* (New York: Oxford University Press, 1970); also Joseph R. Gusfield, "Tradition and Modernity: Misplaced Polarities in the Study of Social Change," *American Journal of Sociology*, vol. 72 (January 1967), pp. 351–62.

5. This and other criticisms will not be new to many students of political development. What is new is the widespread articulation of such views within the Third World. Moreover, this critique of the Western model needs to be presented as a prelude to the discussion of indigenous models that follows. For some earlier critiques of the Western development model, see Wiarda, "Ethnocentrism"; Bendix, "Tradition and Modernity"; Dean C. Tipps, "Modernization Theory and the Comparative Studies of Society: A Critical Perspective," *Comparative Studies of Society and History*, vol. 15 (March 1973), pp. 199–226; C. D. Hah and J. Schneider, "A Critique of Current Theories of Political Development and Modernization," *Social Research*, vol. 35 (Spring 1968), pp. 130–58. See also the statements on the different meanings of democracy by Costa Rican President Luis Alberto Monge and Nigerian President Alhaji Shehu Shagari at the Conference on Free Elections, Department of State, Washington, D.C., November 4–6, 1982; also R. William Liddle, "Comparative Political Science and the Third World," mimeographed (Columbus: Ohio State University, Department of Political Science).

6. An excellent treatment of these themes is Claudio Veliz, *The Centralist Tradition in Latin America* (Princeton, N.J.: Princeton University Press, 1980); also Clifford Geertz, *Negara: The Theatre State in Nineteenth Century Bali* (Princeton, N.J.: Princeton University Press, 1980), in which he shows that the culture and the theater are the substance, not just superstructure.

7. Especially relevant is the general critique of the Western sociological bias in T. O. Wilkinson, "Family Structure and Industrialization in Japan," *American Sociological Review*, vol. 27 (October 1962), pp. 678–82; also Alberto Guerreiro Ramos, "Modernization: Toward a Possibility Model," in *Developing Nations*, ed. Beling and Totten, pp. 21–59; and Gusfield, "Tradition and Modernity."

8. William P. Glade, "Problems of Research in Latin American Studies," in *New Directions in Language and Area Studies* (Milwaukee: University of Wisconsin at Milwaukee for the Consortium of Latin American Studies Programs, 1979), pp. 81–101.

9. Veliz, *The Centralist Tradition*.

10. For a general statement, Leonard S. Binder et al., eds., *Crises and Sequences in Political Development* (Princeton, N.J.: Princeton University Press, 1971).

11. See the classic statement by Marc Bloch, *Feudal Society* (Chicago: University of Chicago Press, 1961).

12. Daniel Bell, *The Coming of Post-Industrial Society* (New York: Basic Books, 1973). On May 26, 1981, in a personal conversation, Professor Bell asserted that by a quite different route he had also "come to similar conclusions regarding the inadequacies of many social science concepts since they derive almost exclusively from a particular Western tradition." Much of the new social science literature emanating from Latin America since the 1960s makes many of the same arguments.

13. The dependency literature is extensive; among the best statements is Fernando Henrique Cardoso and Enzo Faletto, *Dependency and Development in Latin America* (Berkeley: University of California Press, 1978).

14. For a general discussion, S. N. Eisenstadt, "Post-Traditional Societies and the Continuity and Reconstruction of Tradition," *Daedalus*, vol. 102 (Winter 1973), pp. 1–27; and idem, *Modernization: Protest and Change* (Englewood Cliffs, N.J.: Prentice-Hall, 1966).

15. Lloyd I. Rudolph and Susanne Hoeber Rudolph, *The Modernity of Tradition* (Chicago: University of Chicago Press, 1967).

16. The case of Tanzania is especially interesting in this regard.

17. The arguments are detailed in Wiarda, "Ethnocentrism."

18. A more complete discussion with regard to one region is in Howard J. Wiarda, ed., *The Continuing Struggle for Democracy in Latin America* (Boulder, Colo.: Westview Press, 1980).

19. G. A. D. Soares, "Latin American Studies in the United States," *Latin American Research Review* 11 (1976); and Howard J. Wiarda, "Latin American Intellectuals and the 'Myth' of Underdevelopment" (Presentation made at the Seventh National Meeting of the Latin American Studies Association, Houston, November 2–5, 1977, and published in Wiarda, *Corporatism and National Development in Latin America* [Boulder, Colo.: Westview Press, 1981], pp. 236–38.)

20. Susanne J. Bodenheimer, *The Ideology of Developmentalism: The American Paradigm-Surrogate for Latin American Studies* (Beverly Hills, Calif.: Sage, 1971); Teresa Hayter, *Aid as Imperialism* (Baltimore, Md.: Penguin, 1971); Ronald H. Chilcote, *Theories of Comparative Politics: The Search for a Paradigm* (Boulder, Colo.: Westview Press, 1981); Hah and Schneider, "Critique."

21. In a faculty seminar I chaired in 1980–1981 on "New Directions in Comparative Politics" at the Center for International Affairs, Harvard University, several of whose members were part of the original and highly influential SSRC Committee on Comparative Politics, it was striking to note in the occasional seminar remarks by these members how strongly the Cold War ideology of that time pervaded the SSRC Committee's assumptions. One of our seminar members, himself part of the original SSRC Committee, flatly stated that the purpose of this group was to formulate a non-Communist theory of change and thus to provide a non-Marxian alternative for the developing nations. Gabriel A. Almond's now virtually forgotten *The Appeals of Communism* (Princeton, N.J.: Princeton University Press, 1954) was especially important in helping shape this sentiment. In a volume that grows out of this seminar (*New Directions in Comparative Politics*, forthcoming), I have sought to explain the context and biases undergirding the early development literature.

22. Selig S. Harrison, *The Widening Gulf: Asian Nationalism and American Policy* (New York: Free Press, 1978). My critique of the development paradigm is contained in "Is Latin America Democratic and Does It Want to Be? The Crisis and Quest of Democracy in the Hemisphere," in *The Continuing Struggle*, ed. Wiarda, pp. 3–24.

23. Samuel P. Huntington, *Political Order in Changing Societies* (New Haven, Conn.: Yale University Press, 1968); and Wiarda, "Ethnocentrism."

24. See also Sigmund, *Ideologies*. Especially striking are the differences between the old and new editions of this study, and the differences in Sigmund's own thinking as contained in his introductions.

25. Tentatively entitled *Third World Conceptions of Development*, also growing out of the Harvard seminar on "New Directions in Comparative Politics," and under the auspices of AEI.

26. Vrajenda Raj Mehta, *Beyond Marxism: Towards an Alternative Perspective* (New Delhi: Manohar Publications, 1978), p. 12. I am grateful to my colleague Thomas Pantham for bringing this work and the debate that swirls about it to my attention. Subsequent page references to Mehta will be in parentheses in the text. A parallel volume from Latin America is José Arico, *Marx e a America Latina* (Rio de Janeiro: Paz e Terra, 1982).

27. For a critique see Thomas Pantham, "Integral Pluralism: A Political Theory for India?" *India Quarterly* (July-December 1980), pp. 396–405.

28. For another outstanding Indian contribution to the theory of development see Rajni Kothari, *Footsteps into the Future* (New York: Free Press, 1975).

29. G. H. Jansen, *Militant Islam* (New York: Harper and Row, 1980), as well as the special series by Sir Willie Morris in the *Christian Science Monitor*, August-September 1980, and that by Flora Lewis in the *New York Times*, December 1979.

30. An especially good statement is by Harvard anthropologist Mary Catherine Bateson, "Iran's Misunderstood Revolution," *New York Times*, February 20, 1979, p. 14.

31. Jansen, *Militant Islam*; Said, *Orientalism*; Barry Rubin, *Paved with Good Intentions* (New York: Oxford University Press, 1980); Shahrough Akhavi, *Religion and Politics in Contemporary Iran* (Albany: State University of New York Press, 1980); Ali Masalehdan, "Values and Political Development in Iran" (Ph.D. diss., University of Massachusetts at Amherst, 1981); and Michael Fischer, *Iran: From Religious Dispute to Revolution* (Cambridge, Mass.: Harvard University Press, 1980). See also the discussion led by Fischer on "Iran: Is It an Example of Populist Neo-Traditionalism?" Joint Seminar on Political Development (JOSPOD), Cambridge, Mass., Minutes of the Meeting of October 15, 1980.

32. Anwar Syed, *Pakistan: Islam, Politics and National Solidarity* (New York: Praeger, 1982). The implications of Syed's discussion are considerably broader than the case he discusses. See also Inayatullah, *Transfer of Western Development Model to Asia and Its Impact* (Kuala Lumpur: Asian Center for Development and Administration, 1975).

33. David Apter, *Ghana in Transition* (New York: Atheneum, 1967); and Ruth Schachter Morgenthau, "Single Party Systems in West Africa," *American Political Science Review*, vol. 55 (June 1961) have both helped to popularize (and, to a degree, romanticize) the notion of the viability of African single party systems. Henry L. Bretton, *Power and Politics in Africa* (Chicago: Aldine, 1973) helped to explode those myths.

34. My understanding of these currents in Africa has been enriched by various exchanges with and the seminar presentations of Africanist Naomi Chazan, a colleague in both Jerusalem and Cambridge; and by the writings of Swiss sociologist Pierre Pradervand, *Family Planning Programmes in Africa* (Paris: Organization for Economic Cooperation and Development, 1970); and idem, "Africa—The Fragile Giant," a series of articles in the *Christian Science*

Monitor, December 1980. See also Crawford Young, *The Politics of Cultural Pluralism* (Madison: University of Wisconsin Press, 1976).

35. For a partial and inconclusive exchange on this theme see the comments of Susan Bourque, Samuel P. Huntington, Merilee Grindle, Brian Smith, and the author in a JOSPOD seminar on "Neo-Traditionalism in Latin America," in Minutes of the Meeting of November 19, 1980.

36. Louis Hartz et al., *The Founding of New Societies* (New York: Harcourt, Brace, 1964).

37. Howard J. Wiarda, "Spain and Portugal," in *Western European Party Systems*, ed. Peter Merkl (New York: Free Press, 1980), pp. 298–328; and idem, "Does Europe Still Stop at the Pyrenees, or Does Latin America Begin There? Iberia, Latin America, and the Second Enlargement of the European Community," in *The Impact of an Enlarged European Community on Latin America*, ed. Georges D. Landau and G. Harvey Summ (forthcoming); also published under the same title as Occasional Paper no. 2 (Washington, D.C.: American Enterprise Institute for Public Policy Research, January 1982).

38. Wiarda, *Politics and Social Change; Corporatism and Development; The Continuing Struggle*; and (earlier) "Toward a Framework for the Study of Political Change in the Iberic-Latin Tradition: The Corporative Model," *World Politics*, vol. 25 (January 1973), pp. 206–35.

39. José E. Rodó, *Ariel* (Montevideo: Dornaleche y Reyes, 1900); an English translation by F. J. Stimson was published under the same title (Boston: Houghton-Mifflin, 1922).

40. Among others, Veliz, *The Centralist Tradition*; Glen Dealy, *The Public Man: An Interpretation of Latin America and Other Catholic Countries* (Amherst: University of Massachusetts Press, 1977); Leopoldo Zea, *The Latin American Mind* (Norman: University of Oklahoma Press, 1963); Octavio Paz, *The Labyrinth of Solitude* (New York: Grove Press, 1961); Richard M. Morse, "The Heritage of Latin America," in *The Founding*, ed. Hartz.

41. H. G. Creel, *Chinese Thought: From Confucius to Mao Tse-tung* (Chicago: University of Chicago Press, 1963); Stuart H. Schram, *The Political Thought of Mao Tse-tung* (New York: Praeger, 1976).

42. T. O. Wilkinson, *The Urbanization of Japanese Labor* (Amherst: University of Massachusetts Press, 1965); Ezra F. Vogel, *Japan as No. 1* (Cambridge, Mass.: Harvard University Press, 1979); and Peter Berger, "Secularity—West and East" (Paper presented at the American Enterprise Institute Public Policy Week, Washington, D.C., December 6–9, 1982).

43. For example, Stanley Rothman and George W. Breslauer, *Soviet Politics and Society* (St. Paul, Minn.: West, 1978); Archie Brown and Jack Gray, eds., *Political Culture and Political Change in Communist States* (New York: Holmes and Meier, 1978); Jerry F. Hough and Merle Fainsod, *How the Soviet Union Is Governed* (Cambridge, Mass.: Harvard University Press, 1979).

44. See, for instance, Raymond Grew, ed., *Crises of Political Development in Europe and the United States* (Princeton, N.J.: Princeton University Press, 1978); and Charles Tilly, ed., *The Formation of Nation States in Western Europe* (Princeton, N.J.: Princeton University Press, 1975).

45. This is one of the criticisms leveled in Pantham, "Integral Pluralism?"

against Mehta's *Beyond Marxism.*

46. Pradervand, "Africa."

47. Pantham, "Integral Pluralism"; and idem, "Political Culture, Political Structure, and Underdevelopment in India," *Indian Journal of Political Science,* vol. 41 (September 1980), pp. 432–56; also Wiarda, *Corporatism and National Development.*

48. Susan Eckstein, *The Poverty of Revolution: The State and the Urban Poor in Mexico* (Princeton, N.J.: Princeton University Press, 1977); Kenneth F. Johnson, *Mexican Democracy: A Critical View* (Boston: Allyn and Bacon, 1971); Octavio Paz, *The Other Mexico* (New York: Grove Press, 1972).

49. Pradervand, "Africa."

50. Lucian Pye, *Aspects of Political Development* (Boston: Little, Brown, 1966).

51. Immanuel Wallerstein, *The Modern World-System* (New York: Academic Press, 1976).

52. Unless of course a nation is willing to withdraw entirely and consciously into isolation, but as Cambodia illustrates that strategy may not work very well either.

53. These issues are addressed in the introduction to the Portuguese language version of Wiarda, *Corporatism and National Development,* published as *O Modelo Corporativo na América Latina e a Latinoamericanização dos Estados Unidos* (Rio de Janeiro: Ed. Vozes, 1983). For an example of such ambivalence see Norbert Lechner, ed., *Estado y Politica en América Latina* (Mexico City: Siglo Veintiuno Editores, 1981); also Carlos Franco, *Del Marxismo Eurocentrico al Marxismo Latinoamericano* (Lima: Centro de Estudios para el Desarrollo y la Participación, 1981).

54. For a country-by-country analysis combined with a common set of theoretical concepts see Howard J. Wiarda and Harvey F. Kline, *Latin American Politics and Development* (second edition, Boulder, Colo.: Westview Press, 1985).

55. Masalehdan, *Values and Political Development in Iran.*

56. Oswald Spengler, *The Decline of the West* (New York: Knopf, 1932); and much recent literature.

57. See the research agenda as set forth in the edited volumes *New Directions in Comparative Politics* and *Third World Conceptions of Development,* forthcoming.

58. In a personal conversation with the author, December 1979.

59. The research perspectives suggested here and the implications of these as set forth in the concluding paragraphs are explored in greater detail in Wiarda, "Ethnocentrism"; *Politics and Social Change; The Continuing Struggle for Democracy;* and *Corporatism and National Development.*

60. I have attempted to formulate such a theory in "Toward a Framework for the Study of Political Change in the Iberic-Latin Tradition" and in *Corporatism and National Development.*

61. For example, our community development, family planning, agrarian reform, military assistance, labor, economic development, and numerous other foreign aid programs have all been based on the "Western" (that is, U.S. and Northwest Europe) model, which is one key reason, I would argue, that

few of them have worked or produced their anticipated consequences. On this see Robert A. Packenham, *Liberal America and the Third World: Political Development Ideas in Foreign Aid and Social Science* (Princeton, N.J.: Princeton University Press, 1973).

Selected AEI Publications

AEI Associates Program